THE PROCESS OF

BECOMING

A GUIDE TO PERSONAL FULFILLMENT

By

RUDOLPH J. & CORA E. CYPSER

Published by

KIM PATHWAYS

by arrangement with
THE TOWN HOUSE PRESS

Dedicated to
our children

Library of Congress Cataloguing in Publication Data:

Cypser, Rudolph J.
    The process of becoming : a guide to personal fulfillment / by
Rudolph J. & Cora E. Cypser.
        p.   cm.
    Bibliography: p.
    ISBN 0-940-653-16-8.   ISBN 0-940 653-17-6
    1. Conduct of life. 2. Self-realization. 3. Consciousness.
I. Cypser, Cora E.   II. Title.
BJ1581.2.C97   1988
248.4–dc19   88-24963
                                                                  CIP

For more information:
KIM PATHWAYS
101 Young Road
Katonah, NY 10536

CONTENTS

PREFACE

We often are so enthused that we trip over ourselves scrambling after some enticing morsel. And yet, most of us are uncertain of what is really and ultimately fulfilling. Transient and futile pursuits are the normal diet. Disappointments and frustrations with what once seemed to promise fulfillment are common. So, most of us eventually look for some bed-rock on which to build our hopes. We search for some thread of understanding that may lead to more lasting fulfillment and genuine joy in our lives.

Influenced by Teilhard de Chardin, and others who saw the continuing process of creation, one realizes the central importance of the idea of growth in consciousness—particularly empathy, caring love, and kindness. To our surprise, we find that much of our greatest happiness comes from living that way. What this means in the practical, struggling, daily lives of ordinary people, is the first issue. Money, sex, authority, and the common ills of our society, are among the realities that need to be examined in the light of this idea.

Trying then to see a broader perspective, this role of ours in growing consciousness appears to be part of a vast evolutionary creation process. One sees that so much in history can be related to the continuing birth of spirit in humankind, and, as some would say, to the steady birth of the 'Spirit of God' in every human heart. It's as if the Spirit of God is born in the hearts of people as they gradually accept some of God's attributes that are implanted there. All peoples and all religions are concerned with this creative birthing.

Does that spirit slowly permeate the earth, as each individual grows to the point where others can see God's spirit working in them? Certainly, one has to face and overcome the nagging miserableness of life one often finds. Yet, despite that persistent misery, there is a dominant thread of creativity and great joy in this continuing birth of spirit. We suggest that it is the participation in this birthing which brings real purpose to one's life, a solid sense of personal fulfillment and self worth, and genuine happiness.

1

MIND EXPLORATION

1.1 BECOMING AWARE

In seeking personal fulfillment, all of us, sooner or later, experience a nagging desire to get to know ourselves. We want to see more clearly all that makes us what we are, and all that is around us. We want to discover the better realities which, in our haste, we may have ignored. We want to shake off our sleep, to be more aware, and to realize what prisons we may have fashioned for ourselves. To be all that we are capable of being, we intuitively feel that we must have knowledge of what we can be. We want to understand the opportunities we have.

Finding our inner self, - our true self, requires digging through layers of defensive masks and false assumptions. Breaking down old prejudices, discarding old ideas, and acquiring new ideas, can become a glad process of stretching and growth. We're relieved to change old habits of thinking and old habits of feeling.[1] We begin to seek not only a given detail, but the place, the function, and the meaning of this detail in relation to the whole.[2] In doing this, we find ourselves broadening our awareness, making the transition from the particular to the general, from details to the whole, and from the illusory to the real.

We find that we must be open to new understandings and

1

expect new clarity in the future. We may even be startled to find that we need to accept some uncertainty and to adopt new hypotheses. To be comfortable with this, we have to accept the fact that some uncertainty, and hypotheses, are O.K., healthy, and normal. It is not necessary that we now understand completely or absolutely correctly. Our path is dynamic and continually being corrected. We expect, instead, that we will always be growing in awareness and knowledge. The further thrill of discovery and fresh illumination is always waiting. At each step, we can enjoy a quiet happiness when the light suddenly comes on and we have a clearer insight.

To understand, and so grow, is often joyful. However, we find we cannot do it alone, and we seek the wisdom of others to aid us. In this, an analytic frame of mind, and a certain skepticism would also seem to be in order. A little sharpness of our tools for critical analysis would probably help. Therefore, it may be a good investment to take a few minutes, in this first chapter, to examine the nature of the information and knowledge we use.

1.2 LEARNING DESPITE UNCERTAINTY

The acquisition of understanding opens the way to our taking another step in our process of becoming. One feels that a continuing birthing of awareness may lead to true peace of mind. But can we be certain that our understanding is correct?

Sifting Our Sources

Besides our own valuable but limited experience, we have many ways of obtaining inputs from others, such as reading, conversations, arguments, lectures, or television. Most of it is trivial, only temporarily amusing, or outright garbage. But some is precious. The writings of the ancients, that survived over the centuries, are particularly noteworthy. We can ferret out those sources that we believe are more likely to be valuable to us. We can sort out, filter out, and select the parts that fit. Basically, we are looking for the sharing of experience, and sharing the results of reflective thought. We have to be very selective, and at the same time be open to change. In critical reflection, we freely sift, reject some, accept some, gradually building up our own library of things that fit comfortably with our own experience and judgements.

Still, we are uncertain. We try to verify. We continually test the knowledge we use to see if it still holds. However, that verification is itself often elusive. What do we mean by verification anyway? Lonergan puts it realistically:

> To reach knowledge, to discern between astronomy and astrology, chemistry and alchemy, history and legend, philosophy and myth, there are needed the further activities of reflecting, doubting, marshaling and weighing the evidence, and judging. Finally this process of judging, ... is like scientific verification, not as verification is imagined by the naive to be a matter of looking, peering, intuiting, but as verification in fact is found to be, namely, a cumulative convergence of direct and indirect confirmations, any one of which, by itself, settles just nothing.[3]

The Range of Uncertainty

Much of our quest seems to be to reduce the elements of uncertainty in our lives. We analyze and test in a perpetual search for true knowledge, accuracy, and the elimination of doubt. Yet, there always seems to be a limit, beyond which we cannot yet go. How certain can we be that our knowledge is correct, accurate, and undistorted? Perhaps, one hopes, some kinds of knowledge, at least, are 100% 'true', like the sciences, for example. Or are they? Of course not. Some physicists once thought, around the turn of the century, that the laws of physics were well understood, and there was not much more to learn. Since then, many of their hypotheses have been proven to be wrong or at least inadequate or inaccurate in many cases. As time passes, new vistas of knowledge are added, which may clarify or give an entirely new perspective or even contradict earlier knowledge.

Even the science of measurement reflects this fact. We're accustomed to saying we measure something only to a 'tolerance' of, - for example, plus or minus one thousandth of an inch. In this regard, an interesting conclusion was made by a physicist named Heisenberg. In his attempts to measure properties of tiny particles, he realized that there is a definite limit to the possible accuracy of measurement. In fact, if one tries to get very precise in the measurement of our tiniest particles, then the very attempt to measure affects the properties one is trying to measure! The now famous Heisenberg Uncertainty Principle says that some degree of uncertainty is always a fact of physics. If that's true in the sciences, then perhaps some degree of uncertainty is also a fundamental and necessary part of life in general. At least, that seems to be our experience. A prudent assumption would seem to be that uncertainty is a fact of life, and perhaps we had better become accustomed to it. We had better realize that everything we 'know' is only known to a degree, with some range of uncertainty (or tolerance) of that knowledge. It may simply be unclear, misinterpreted, or distorted by our own inadequacies. But to us it is not one hundred percent accurate. There is always room for further clarification, refinement, and understanding; this seems to apply to our most cherished beliefs.

The Matter of Viewpoint

Another aspect of uncertain knowledge has to do with viewpoint. We each see things from a particular vantage point; and we often don't understand that others can legitimately see things differently. There's so much truth in that old Buddhist story about the five blind Indians who approached an elephant.

> One, grasping the leg, said: "It's like a tree."
> Another, grasping the tail, said: "It's like a rope."
> Another, feeling it's side, said: "It's like a wall."
> Another, feeling the trunk, said: "It's like a snake."
> The last, feeling the ear, said: "It's like a fan."

Were they all wrong, or were they all partly right? How often our own arguments are similar! If only we could remember that we all see only partially. Moreover, *multiple differing viewpoints can be helpful!*

The Sense of Exposure

Msgr. George Higgins makes a related point:

> The basic precondition of liberal tolerance is an appreciation of our own ignorance. We have to recognize that, on virtually any point at all, the most knowledgeable of us may be wrong. Here, however, we confront a psychological impulse

Figure 1: The Blind Men and the Elephant

> common to us all. We are unwilling to face the fact of the
> unknown because it fills us with fear or imposes on us the
> strain of perplexing uncertainty.[4]

Many people are not comfortable unless they believe that most
things are known with absolute accuracy and finality. Somewhere, they would like to think, there is someone who is not beset
with uncertainty. They'd rather not think that their doctor is
somewhat uncertain about his diagnosis. They'd rather assume
that our president has complete understanding of the economy
and foreign affairs. A high degree of trust in our 'experts' is
certainly helpful, up to a point. On the other hand, beyond that
point, might it not be more prudent to recognize the uncertainty in
all endeavors? Facing that reality may be difficult. But one cannot
really live comfortably with unreality. In the long run, facing
reality may avoid some catastrophic false dependencies.

We all tend to become somewhat myopic, living in a limited
knowledge world, - in a mere bubble within reality. To break out,
into a larger sphere, we often need to venture into uncertain
waters. We also need to dare to distrust what knowledge we have
been holding onto. We need to question and reexamine even our
long accepted beliefs.

There's an exposure. We're bound to make somewhat inaccurate and incomplete conclusions. It seems inevitable that we will
make some mistakes. So be it. That is better than blind ignorance
and delusion. We seek the very best sources we can; we try to be
open to change, despite prior presumptions, prior biases, and
intolerances. We continue the search, trusting that this search
eventually, by zigs and zags, will find a better path. Our tree of
knowledge, it seems, is seldom completely discredited; the root
and parts of the trunk seem solid enough. So what if some
seemingly healthy branches succumb to decay! We trust that our
knowledge will continue to grow along some other main-stem
path; and we'll find it.

As we search for learning and understanding, we can find in
that searching a sense of adventure and accomplishment. It seems
that coping with the element of uncertainty is a part of life that
makes use of our inherent humanity; it enables us to grow and to
be fully human. Another level of capability has been reached with
the realization that uncertainty can be coped with effectively.
There is security in that realization. Each day can then become
part of a never ending voyage of discovery.

1.3 MODELS AND HYPOTHESES

But how can we depend on knowledge if we're so uncertain of it? In fact, we operate all the time (usually without realizing it) on the basis of approximate knowledge. "It's about three o'clock," we say. And then we proceed to act on that knowledge, because it often doesn't matter if our time knowledge is a little bit off. That clock is a neat representation of the day, isn't it? We note that its hands go around twice in twenty four hours, which is just the same measure as the actual time of our day. The clock is a 'model' of the way time passes. Most clocks used to be 'off' a little bit; but that usually didn't matter. Thus, it seems that models are common, - almost a 'way of life', because approximate models are very practical and useful. This is the case in both the physical and the philosophical realms.

The Physical Realm

We build a model of a bridge before we build the bridge, to determine probable stresses, and to help in the design. The model is only approximate because it would be impractical to put all the detail in the model. Besides, there's a limit to our knowledge of how to represent the bridge in infinite detail. Nevertheless, the approximate model is extremely useful. It's not the only possible model; probably, it's not even the most accurate. But it serves our purpose; we even stake our lives on it as we use the resulting bridge.

In the case of things we cannot even see, tentative models are even more important. Take the model of the atom, for example. A big step forward was made when a physicist named Bohr defined his model, with electrons spinning in defined orbits around a nucleus, which had several kinds of particles in it. That model enabled us to correctly predict all kinds of physical behavior, and to do many useful things. Later, however, it was shown that the Bohr model did not always correctly represent the observed reality, and a very different approach to the model was achieved. Another physicist, named Schroedinger, described the components of the atom in terms of wave equations, and expressed the properties of the model in terms of probabilities. So, too, we suggest, all of our models need to evolve, and sometimes to change radically. This should not disturb us, but be accepted realistically.

Lonergan sums up the models of science neatly:

> Modern Science is not true; it is only on the way towards truth. It is not certain; for its positive affirmation it claims no more than probability. It is not knowledge but hypothesis, theory, system, the best available scientific opinions of the day. Its object is not necessity but verified possibility.[5]

Our lives, in fact, are filled with approximate models of realities we only partly understand. The models of the world-economy used by financial institutions have their counterparts in the simple models we usually have in mind for our local banking system. We are content with a relatively superficial idea of how it works, but the important thing is that it works for us.

The Philosophical Realm

Can we not say the same thing about the philosophies that guide our personal lives? As we learn more about the meaning, purpose, direction, and basic goals of our lives, are we, in effect, fashioning only approximate and evolving models of reality? Of course we are; and that's O.K. It would be contrary to the nature of our universe if it were otherwise. Each model appears to be based on a hypothesis. Knowing that new knowledge is very likely to call for modifications of our model, we'd best not pretend that it's the last word. Nevertheless, even the old hypothesis was extremely useful. It seems, that it's quite necessary, and quite ordinary, to accept philosophical hypotheses and their approximate models, and to take action using them, even though we're very aware of the uncertainty involved. Very often, we can act with the assurance that the approximate model is sufficiently accurate for our purposes at the present time.

It's also interesting when two apparently conflicting models are both used to good effect. The particle and wave theories of matter and radiation are good examples; the two models are completely different, and yet both appear to be 'true' in that they correctly describe and predict behavior in a wide range of circumstances. Another example that comes to mind is the 'personal' model of God common in the west versus the apparently 'impersonal' model favored by some Buddhists of the east. Again, recognizing a certain humility concerning our models, is it even possible that the reality is expressible, at least partially, by both models? Is it possible that the reality is greater than either model and yet served well by both? We think that's probable, given the elements of uncertainty in all of our knowledge and the necessary limits to the completeness of all of our models.

Therefore, most knowledge that is conceptual ideas (as distinct from factual events), is also best thought of in terms of one or more hypotheses. Hypotheses and models of reality are common and necessary for us to function; hence, it is not surprising that they are also essential to any philosophy of living, and many aspects of theology, too.

We must try to be realistic. We confidently use and depend on all kinds of hypotheses and models, because we need to see a purpose in our lives. We need to see ourselves within some larger conceptual framework that makes sense and gives our lives meaning. On the other hand, though it is sometimes disconcerting, we have to accept the fact that every hypothesis is subject to clarification or improvement, if not replacement. Basically, we have to accept that element of uncertainty; and we become comfortable with that state of affairs. Hence, as we put together hypotheses about the meaning of life, we gladly accept the fact that hypotheses can be very useful and can contribute to genuine happiness, even if they are not perfect or unique.

1.4 MODES OF EXPRESSION

Another factor, which requires that we treat knowledge with care and imagination, is the inherent limitations in most forms of expression. We always use a kind of short-hand notation. For example, the road-sign of a circle and bar is well known to mean 'no admittance', but thirty years ago it wouldn't have been recognized. There are multiple interpretations. Sculptures, abstract art, and even words can convey multiple meanings. Consider, furthermore, that the picture of your boy friend or girl friend brings many associations to mind. The picture doesn't tell everything about your friend, but it's a symbol that conveys a great deal (even though it might also be misleading). Maybe a word-picture would have been able to convey almost as much information, as words can also be very effective symbols of a greater reality. They all, however, have limitations.

Symbols

Symbols are sometimes very precise. When we say, " $1 + 1 = 2$,"
there is not much uncertainty in what we mean. But when we
say, "We are all one," that could mean a variety of things. It even
seems that our symbols become less precise as the message
becomes more complex and meaningful. In general, for profound
subjects, even our best words fail us; we have to admit that words
can only convey approximately what we mean. *Many times, the
words are inadequate*; they convey only a part of the total. Then, too,
the words that we choose, are words that we are familiar with,
comfortable with, and are meaningful to us. That means, unfortunately, that our expression is colored by our limitations, experiences, and culture. It follows that *every set of words (symbols) used
by others are likewise limited, convey only a portion of the reality they try
to convey, and are colored by the author's culture.* Every translation,
too, multiplies the uncertainty; the culture of the translator is
often different from that of the author, and subtle changes in word
meanings and inferences have occurred. Very different messages
often result. There is nothing malicious in this; it's just the nature
of things; and perhaps it is better if we accept this.

Even our best authors are limited by the language used; and
their expressions are only stepping stones for our understanding
of the full reality. Perhaps we should realize, then, that all forms
of communication, like the examples above, can be symbols of
something greater, something beyond the mechanism of communication. Thus, these symbols have something in common
with the hypotheses and models we discussed earlier. Both are not
the reality themselves, but only partial representations of some
greater reality beyond. The human mind can and must extrapolate
beyond the symbols if further understanding is to be obtained.
That may seem troubling, but there's also excitement and pleasure
in that use of the mind.

If all of our words, pictures, models, and so forth, may be
only incomplete intermediaries, we might have to be careful not to
mistake them for the reality itself. Worse, still, we might easily
presume that the representation was the precise reality, when, as
we surmised before, there probably is considerable uncertainty in
just what the reality is. On the other hand, realizing all this gives
one a certain necessity to explore with the mind to find greater
depths of understanding. We are inherently free to do this, and
thus to use some of the best gifts given to humanity. That seems

to be how we are made; it's by such exploration, projection, and use of our imagination that we grow, become fully human, and find further fulfillment.

Idols

Another interesting example of symbols is the subject of statues in churches. They clearly can be symbols. But if one forgot that they were representations of something beyond, if one focused on the statue instead of what it represents, one would be accused of idolatry. Some of us tended to think of idolatry as we watched people paying homage before various statues, which were referred to as gods, in a Hindu temple. However, we had to reconsider our opinion when a Hindu guide explained that people use these symbols as a way to the one true God which they know little about. Again, it would seem, the charge of idolatry would be justified only if the worshipers did not realize they were using symbols as representations of a greater reality beyond. Couldn't that same mistake, perhaps, be made with symbols of various types, and various degrees of abstraction? A related form of idolatry may be a danger with representations or symbols ranging from the golden calf to holy books and to any particular idea or expression of prized concepts. *In a sense, we might be guilty of a kind of idolatry whenever we close our minds to the greater reality beyond the symbol or model, and act as if they were the reality itself.*

For example, suppose some gifted person or group tries to express (in words of his times and culture) a concept that is truly profound, whose full scope is only partially comprehended by the speaker. That partial expression may be an extremely valuable interim symbol or model of the full reality. However, one could idolize that gifted expression, if one insisted that it were the full and final expression applicable to all situations, forgetting that it is only a symbol of a truth or wisdom much greater than the expression. In such cases, the early expression should be recognized as an aid to understanding, rather than the full truth itself. *The concepts are means to an end, and not the end itself.* That we often lose sight of the inherent limitations in many concepts, models, or sets of symbols, is painfully evident from the absolute certainty and even militancy with which they are usually professed. One must wonder how many arguments might have been avoided if this perspective, concerning the limitations and intermediary nature of models, were prevalent at the time.

Religious symbols, in particular, are often used to represent a reality that is beyond the limits of possible experience.[6] It doesn't matter that they are 'only' symbols; they can have great effect. Such symbols can activate the human mind to begin processing the ideas which are beyond the symbols. That reality is thus communicated through the symbols and is experienced in them. On the negative side, such symbols can also become simply mysterious and confusing. In ancient times, in particular, they further served to enhance an elite who employed the symbols to control others. Despite such misuse, however, we've got to recognize the positive power and beauty that symbols can have when used in a constructive manner.

Cultural Differences

One has to be amused as well as intrigued by how different literatures in different times make use of different levels of abstraction and indirection. For example, in eastern and mid-eastern cultures, we are more likely to find use of metaphors, allegories and analogies. Sometimes, also, knowledge is trans-mitted by the use of myths. All are extremely useful, but also offer possibilities for distortion of the intended message.

Another almost lost art is that of the parable, a form of story telling, involving a teaching in which the listeners take part. Here the message is obviously not in the precise events of the story, but in what the story brings to mind in the imagination of the listeners. The exact conclusion is dependent, in part, on the listener. It is a form of teaching that introduces a concept and then is particularly open to interpretations, depending on the various circumstances of the participants. In some cultures, this is made more complex by the use of double meanings, where, for example, ancient phrases are employed in new settings, and the ancient associations (which were well known at the time of writing) add another stimulating message to the more obvious one.

In commenting on some parts of the New Testament, Knitter observes interestingly that:

> Some knowledge is better understood not as photographs, but as impressionistic paintings. It may be conditioned by its historico-cultural context and concerns; it may make use of mythic models or symbolic images drawn from its environ-

ment. These images, like all mythic-symbolic language, are not to be taken literally, but they are to be taken seriously.[7]

A related variable is the force of expression used by people in different cultures. Before the advent of the printing press, people had to memorize large quantities of information. Histories, laws, religious customs and rituals all had to be memorized. People knew that memory was best when images were associated with emotions and drama. Hence there was an inclination to express things dramatically and with extremes. Similarly, in the middle east, one's strong conviction on a subject is more likely to be indicated by an exaggeration, or by emphasizing an unrealizable ideal, or by taking an extreme position, - for example, "So if your right eye causes you to sin, take it out and throw it away!" (Matthew 5:29-30). That type of statement conveys a direction, is so understood in that culture, and is not meant to be taken literally.

Finally, in ordinary, everyday life, we find that the words and body-language, employed in any discussion, are only part of the message. We always have to look beyond, and stand in the shoes of the presenter, to try to understand the full intent.

The Search

As we try to absorb literature that uses such expressions, we need to be careful to understand what level of abstraction we are at, and from which culture it comes, and to distinguish these from the distant reality that the expressions represent. This process proves to be very interesting and often difficult; and much confusion between symbols and the reality they represent has resulted. At the same time, to ignore such literature would be an incredible waste; those who went before us gave so much to enrich us; we must try to discern their intended meanings. We can grow in our own personhood with the aid of their hard-won understanding; the inspiration and awakening we can get are well worth the effort. The exercise of the imagination in doing this is thus part of the pleasurable process of broadening our awareness, and hence of our becoming a whole person.

1.5 EXTRASENSORY SOURCES OF KNOWLEDGE ?

We like to pride ourselves on accepting only knowledge that is perceived by our five senses. This, then, is demonstrable. But is

there reality beyond our senses? How could this be? Just to
illustrate this possibility, consider a blind caterpillar, living on a
telephone wire. All his life, he just goes up and down that wire.
For him, there is only one dimension (or possibly two) in the
universe. His senses and all his experiences give few clues that
there are three dimensions in space. And yet, there are. So, too,
with our senses, perhaps. We have only five. Could we use more?
Isn't it just as possible that there could be a reality beyond what we
can sense?

We live in the four dimensions of space and time. We think
only in terms of space and time. If we try to comprehend other
dimensions, we have great difficulty. (To illustrate other dimensions, we can imagine our realm of space and time to form a plane;
and then we might imagine other levels of existence in other
planes above or below ours.[8] Whatever the image, we begin to
recognize the possibility of other levels of existence and our
possible relationship to those other levels.)

This, we are inclined to protest, seems to violate our laws of
physics. However, we also realize that all the laws of physics are
not known to us. Science has taught us that these laws change
dramatically at the boundaries of our knowledge.[9] For example,
the theory of relativity explains that time shrinks and expands in
the region of the speed of light. So also does space. These
phenomena have been confirmed in astronomical observations.
Moreover, at the other end of the space dimension, in the nucleus
of the atom, we have had to accept the startling quantum theory.
Here the continuity of things disappears, and energy levels have
leaped to establish separate stable states. These further demonstrate that we continually have much to learn about the realms of
reality. Therefore, the hypothesis of other levels of existence,
which we do not yet clearly perceive, should not be completely
ruled out on the basis of ordinary physics.

Frequently, we hear of extrasensory experiences. A friend of
ours was having a truly terrible personal heartache, one night,
because of the infidelity of her husband. Early the next morning,
she received a frantic phone call from a very dear and distant
friend, asking what was wrong. Her friend, too, had had a most
distressing night. She just knew that our friend was in agony, and
also knew that it concerned the husband, even though the trouble
had been a completely kept secret. Such 'clairvoyance' is not
uncommon; but it is not under our control. It's a clear indication
of some extrasensory communication, but we don't really compre-

hend it. Nevertheless, the fact that such subjects defy measurement, and are difficult to verify by experiment, does not mean that they are unreal, unimportant, or unworthy of study.

To be realistic, it seems we have to admit that we know very little about extrasensory perceptions; but *they very probably do exist*, judging from our own experiences, despite the primitive state of our own knowledge. Many, indeed, believe in a reality beyond our senses; one 'place' or 'space' associated with that reality, some call heaven. The existence of personalities similar to ours, and much beyond ours, in this other realm, is also a common belief. It is conceivable, then, that valuable information and guidance might come from such an 'extrasensory source'. We need to approach this possibility with an open mind, but with caution.

In this connection, one needs to periodically reexamine the idea of 'God', and the nature of 'faith', and what these mean in current experience. These concepts have matured gradually over the millennia, and seem to go through a constant (though slow) clarification, reinterpretation in the light of current problems, adaptation to the needs of different cultures, and even the dropping of certain beliefs. In all this, it's sometimes popular to speak of the 'death of God'; for it's most appropriate and necessary to periodically discard some time-honored adornments. However, change is usually beneficial; and we would rather interpret that same process as the constant birth of the concept of God, - in some ways the same, but always clarified. We'll address these issues further in later chapters.

1.6 FINDING OUR WAY

The world is in a stage of information explosion and accelerating technological advances. The growth of the human person, that must wisely manage these resources, must keep pace. To help do this, the slow, erratic, but steady gathering of knowledge, understanding, and wisdom must be vigorously pursued. A central part of this must be the very philosophy of life itself. Who are we? What is our purpose? How can we best achieve fulfillment? We have many different sources of knowledge and understanding, all of which have their peculiarities and uncertainties. One happy fact gives us all encouragement; we have been blessed with a variety of tools for building creatively. Humankind's gifts of imagination, and powers of discernment and discovery, are exciting and full of promise, despite many uncertainties. The best minds in the world have been using these capabilities for thousands of years. This discernment of ourselves and our direction is the golden opportunity that must always be seized, if each of us is to become what we can be, and to do our small part to aid the continued growth of ourselves and the species.

REFERENCES

[1]P. D. Ouspensky, *The Fourth Way*, Vintage Books, New York, 1971, p. 276.

[2]*ibid.*, p. 47.

[3]B.J.F. Lonergan, "The Dehellenization of Dogma", *Theological Studies*, June, 1967, Woodstock, Md.

[4]George G. Higgins, "The Social Mission of the Church After Vatican II", *America*, July 26, 1986, p. 27.

[5]Bernard Lonergan, "Dimensions of Meaning", *Collection*, Herder and Herder, N.Y., 1967, p. 259.

[6]E.A. Johnson, "The Symbolic Character of Theological Statements About Mary", *Journal of Ecumenical Studies*, Vol. 22, number 2, Spring 1985, pp. 312–336.

[7]Paul F. Knitter, *No Other Name?*, Orbis Books, Maryknoll, N.Y., 1985, p.180.

[8]Huston Smith, *Forgotten Truth*, Harper and Row, New York, 1977, p. 24.

[9]*ibid.* pp. 84–85.

2

TO BE SOMEBODY

If we are to search for fulfillment, perhaps we'd best first get some idea of what we are; try to shape some kind of hypothesis on what we are destined to become; and try to discern what we want to have as the meaning and purpose of our lives. What does it mean to "be somebody"?

2.1 CONSCIOUSNESS

Evolution

One of the more interesting hypotheses, that affects our sense of what we are, is that of evolution. Based on incomplete but fairly comprehensive evidence, this theory depicts the world in a process of change, over billions of years. The startling conclusion, by many thinkers, is that the change is still going on, and has a direction, - towards increasing complexity. A corollary is that the increasing complexity is accompanied by *increasing consciousness*, involving ever more sophisticated cooperation among components.

The notion of 'consciousness' has to be greatly broadened to take into account the vast differences in matter: molecules, cells,

Figure 2a: The Ascent of Human Consciousness

insects, animals, and mankind.[1-4] Proceeding gradually, and then in quantum jumps, this consciousness takes on dramatically more complex characteristics, as evolution unfolds. Primitive cooperations among cells, and then shared responsibilities in communities of insects, are followed by almost human-like caring and sharing in families of some animals. The most recent quantum jump, to the reflective man, brings the capability for selfless or caring love which has deeper and broader dimensions. This gradual evolution of consciousness is a hypothesis that can have tremendous impact on the meaning of our lives and on the roles we play. One's consciousness apparently can be sharpened by acts of will. On the other hand, unfortunately, consciousness can be allowed to slip back to an animal-like level. We can choose our personality, at least to some extent, to be in tune with this evolution of consciousness or to oppose it.

The Highest Levels of Consciousness

Human consciousness can have many colors. When one person loves another, there can be reverence for the other's personhood, appreciation of the sheer internal as well as external beauty of the person, a realization of the further growth potential of the other, and a desire to maximize the good and the growth of the other. The Greeks even had three words for our word love: eros, filios, and agape. Roughly, eros represented the psychic urge to reach out and relate to another, as well as the spirit of togetherness to be found in sensuality, celebration, and sexual love. Filios represented the sense of common heritage and common bonds, being of a common creation, the brotherhood of all humankind, members of a common family, and brotherly love. Agape stood for the deepest relationship. It involves really understanding the other, and such a close association with another as to be willing to sacrifice one's own interest in favor of the other's.[5] We are primarily concerned with agape, as the greatest love a human can have; but agape may be accompanied by or spring from eros and filios as well. Agape love can have many associates. For simplicity, we'll refer to that composite agape as *caring love*.

Caring love involves decision and effort. It means giving to another, - gladly, and not just from one's surplus. It means reducing the benefit to one's self, or at least expending one's energies in favor of benefiting another. Strangely, this is usually an exhilarating experience that enlarges rather than diminishes; many would say that there is no higher joy and sense of achievement in life than this. Practicing caring love, and thus nurturing others, is the best example we have of enlightened self-interest. In this practice we stretch ourselves; we grow. Thus we find we're exhilarated and rewarded with longer lasting joy. *Empathy, we think, is the peak achievement in consciousness.* It is the ability to put yourself 'in the other person's shoes', to understand where he or she comes from, to realize the other's needs, and finally to feel the other's joys and sorrows, almost as if they were your own. Empathy rests on respect for the other, and an appreciation of the other's inherent or potential worth. Acts of kindness (for example, compassion, tenderness, clemency, gentleness, generosity, and so forth) spring from empathy and caring love. To be fully effective, empathy must apply to all persons. It can apply despite distractions of poverty, poor dress, poor education, physical disability, and differences in race or religion. In short, empathy can concern itself with the inner person and not with the coverings.

Referring back to the Greek ideas of love as eros, filios, and agape, we find empathy in all three. One might say, in fact, that empathy is the heart of agape; empathy is the foundation of filios, and eros is best when it is guided by empathy.

The highest levels of consciousness need to be experienced to be understood and appreciated. Hearing about them or even seeing their effect on others does not suffice. Fortunately, almost everyone has a taste of empathy, caring love, and kindness along the way. That taste must be deliberately savored, however, if the full realization of their value is to be perceived. The taste is wonderful.

Human consciousness can have great breadth, in part because we are able to perceive *in space and in time*. Events and persons, near and far removed, around the world and beyond, plus situations of all kinds in the distant past, the present, or remote future, all can be perceived. Awareness of the local space and the present time can be conditioned by awareness of the beyond. Relationships, particularly with other persons, and groups of persons, are similarly conditioned by this multidimensional awareness. Levels of consciousness can expand, from concern for immediate survival, to concern for others, both now and in the future. *The highest levels of consciousness, then, are*

Figure 2b: To Maximize Consciousness Over Space and Time

characterized by empathy, caring love, and kindness, in a broad sweep of space and time. Maximizing the good over some space may require our personal sacrifice in order to benefit another. Maximizing the good over future time will often involve action today; however, that action may not promise satisfaction today; in fact, it is likely to be a more or less painful payment, - an investment, so to speak, for a return in the future. Our greater fulfillment, over that time span, thus requires the ability to defer gratification, and even to suffer early in order to obtain greater rewards later. All this we can do; these are the proud capabilities of humankind; but no one claims it's easy.

In the relatively short time of human existence (a few million years), it appears that this capability for reflective thought and space/time consciousness has grown. The increase in the sheer size of the human brain, over several millions of years, is cited as a corollary of this. The hypothesis of evolution in consciousness goes even further. It opens the possibility of future growth in consciousness, and in the capacity for selflessness, which optimizes love over space and time. All of creation is still 'in the process of birth'. It is startling to appreciate that we may be the result of evolution from fish. Obviously, if that's the way it was, those fish had little conception of the advanced stages that have since been reached. Similarly, we can hardly conceive of the advanced stages that may be still to come. Nevertheless, we can see the general direction in which we have evolved thus far. A major difference, now, is that we ourselves can partially control the environment that affects our change! Everyone can contribute to his or her own development of consciousness, to the total environment, and hence to that worldwide birthing of empathetic consciousness! That's both consoling and motivating.

To thus grow is to change; and change is often so very painful. As we evolve our individual consciousness, we often need to give up older ideas, patterns of behavior, even what we once accepted as goals. It's often said more dramatically, - we must continually die to self, in order to be born anew into a better state. This periodic giving up of something important really hurts; but the consequent joy and satisfaction of a fuller life also seem to be well worth the price. Each person, then, is still becoming. Every person is valuable, at least in the potential he or she possesses to become a true person, - operating in triumph at the highest levels of consciousness of which we are capable.

2.2 THE ESSENCE OF PERSONHOOD

The Process of Becoming

Becoming a person is an impressively long process. The stream of life, we know, comes to each of us across many generations, through both parents, in the form of DNA and the code of life. These carry the potential for increased consciousness. The DNA codes, apparently, are evolved across the millennia. In a sense, our lives begin back there, at all the contributors to that stream. Then, our own unique code is set for us at conception, but that is still only a potential, and the creation of consciousness continues further. The time when a child has the 'use of reason', and is able to take full responsibility for his or her actions, has been thought to be about the age of seven, when the Catholic church recommends the sacrament of reconciliation.[6] Moreover, the courts grant 'youthful-offender' status, and lighter sentences, to criminals under the age of 18, on the theory that they are not yet mature. Still, we all know middle-aged people who are not yet mature either. Some, who were battered children, may have been prevented from maturing. It seems, therefore, that we are all in a very long process of becoming, both before our birth and then throughout our lives; and some of us mature towards full personhood more rapidly than others.

In particular, we become aware that each of us is the product of the lives and the struggles of a long line of our ancestors, - our parents, grandparents, great-grandparents, and on back ten, a hundred, a thousand generations. They all struggled to survive and to make their lives worthwhile, as best they understood it. They each probably strove to pass on to the next generation something they had gained or learned. It's like each of us is the prow of a great ship which is our heritage extending back in time. If their spirits are somehow still in existence, then, we suspect, they all are rooting for each of us now. In some way, their heritage and their hopes support us. We each, therefore, have a responsibility to those that went before us to make the most of the opportunities they labored to give to us. We each also have an obligation to ourselves, to become as full a person as we possibly can.

In this wonderful on-going creation that is humankind, the

most cherished thing that we can influence is consciousness. As we study, the possibility of this change begins to dawn on us. We realize that, in part, we are like a machine, but we are able to modify the machine, and steer the machine into a direction we choose. Attaining consciousness, then, is connected with the gradual liberation from complete mechanicalness. It includes a realization of our purpose in life, a determination to pursue some 'fundamental options' that we choose to govern our lives, and the fuller use of our capacities for higher level qualities like empathy, caring love, and kindness.

Our Identity

In the pursuit and exercise of this full personhood, one seeks not only quiet satisfaction, but also a zest for living, - a love of life itself. Living fully also means to appreciate beauty wherever it can be found, and to exercise the capacities we have for creativity. We can be mechanical and unthinking or we can enjoy being creative as we tend a garden, build a chair, attract a new client, write, day-dream, study, sing, dance, or paint. We can be creative, too, in justice-making, compassion, forgiveness, and in being kind. In fact, we've all experienced that most activities can be creative and artistic. The degree of creativity depends on how much we draw upon inner resources, how much we intellectually 'process' the subject, and how much energy we invest in it. In all of this, there can be a 'fundamental option' of building the kind of identity we want. Then we make each creative process contribute to the building of that identity. Thus, the most creative, and most important work we can do is to steadily exercise our freedom of choice and creativity in helping to create ourselves.

What then, is the general nature of the identity we want? We seek an identity based in part on what we hold to be truly valuable. We orient that identity towards some ideal that we believe is worth striving for. The ideal must be at least partly achievable. It is not necessarily static, and will usually mature as we grow and our perspective changes. Then, if we are serious about it, we devote time and energy to it. The pursuit of that ideal, and the accompanying evolution of that identity, builds self respect, purpose, and meaning. However, that self respect comes only if our approaching identity merits respect, in our personal judgment.

Our chosen identity, in fact, may be our best view of

ourselves, somewhere between reality and our ideal. The protection of our identity, and hence the preservation of our sense of being whole, demands that we resolutely seek the achievement of our ideal. When we yield ourselves to something that is contrary to our chosen identity, - say, anger or some self indulgence, for example, then we, in effect, exchange our identity for that other level. The pressures of our culture, in fact, may constantly encourage such an exchange of our identity, so as to better conform to the norms of the day.

Our image of ourselves may also suffer under the impact of constant put-downs. The person with dyslexia who therefore can't read is constantly reminded of that unfortunate inability. The student who doesn't do well in test-passing is wrongly categorized as inferior and carries that burden into life. The prison guard who delights in treating prisoners as sub-humans, the boss who continually belittles the employee, the husband who psychologically abuses his wife, and those who constantly criticize others, all help to tear down people's self image. For most people, it's a struggle to maintain that sense of dignity that is so essential to personal motivation and fulfillment. Preserving our identity, then, is a never ending battle. On the other hand, being a co-creator of ourselves is also an opportunity and a responsibility; and it also can be a delight. How could life be boring and superficial if we in fact can help to fashion ourselves?

The Leading Edge

Our ideal may be anything, from the trivial and the ridiculous to the profound. In a broad view, what ought it to be? Returning to our scenario on evolution, each person is the tip of the arrow, the most recent and the leading edge of an ancient process resulting in growth of consciousness. To participate and to contribute to this process, we suggest, is our purpose and our destiny. In this hypothesis, a person lives fully, and achieves his full potential, only to the extent that he uses, and even extends, his capacity for full consciousness. That full consciousness involves an extended capacity for empathy, caring love, and kindness. To approach this ideal is what we mean when we speak of achieving full personhood.

We are not talking about seeking to be loved. On the contrary, seeking to be loved can become selfish and ultimately self destructive. However, we all find that when one nurtures others unselfishly, then that caring love transforms the server, and that attracts the love of others. Thus, the end result is not only the growth of the server, but also the gift of love, from others, that was not sought.

In the exercise of this personhood, one uses the capacity to decide. First there is the decision to be aware of one's self, to have an identity, and to become something; then there's the decision to follow the ideal of being a loving person; and then there are the innumerable decisions, in specific instances, to follow that resolve, and to maximize love in each situation. This, then, is one definition of the essence of personhood, and the purpose and meaning of life:

> To decisively use and extend our capacity for full consciousness, and so to contribute to the plan for evolutionary progress.

Maximizing this good in space and time seems to be like seeking the path of steepest ascent on a mountain. Do we go mostly east and a little south, or due south, or where? Each decision involves many variables, and many consequences. If we were a computer, we might check the effects of changes in each of the variables, in space and time, and then select those changes in each variable so that the combined effects, over some future time, would yield the maximum 'benefits'. In practice, we guess a lot about which course is 'best'. We take small steps 'going up', and correct as we go, to find the best path, which seems to maximize empathy, caring love and kindness in all the space and time we can comprehend. This, it seems, is the search for the path to the fulfillment of humankind's destiny. It is, we suggest, the way to personal joy and fulfillment as well.

As we look back, we can see that each generation has worked on this 'path seeking', with many a 'pioneer' choosing the path that then seemed to use his or her full consciousness. Despite frequent suffering, this course has produced much joy. Though scarcely perceptible, at times, the continued growth of the consciousness of the average inhabitant of earth, is a hope we hang onto. That this growth will continue to occur, in parallel with the awesome technological advances we see all around us, is the basic hope of the future. We find that when they think about it, most persons are determined to participate in and contribute their small bit to this movement. Hoping to operate at the 'leading edge', they strive to 'be somebody' in their daily lives, by being the kind of person that really matters in the grand scheme of things. In this way, they reinforce their vital sense of self worth. They find their place in this vast creation process, which contributes greatly to their renewed sense of purpose, their peace of mind, and their being at home in the universe.

REFERENCES

[1]W. Henry Keney, *A Path Through Teilhard's Phenomenon*, Pflaum Press, Dayton, Ohio, 1970.

[2]Teilhard De Chardin, *Building the Earth*, Avon Books, N.Y., N.Y., 1969.

[3]Teilhard De Chardin, *The Divine Milieu*, Harper Torchbooks, N.Y., N.Y., 1965.

[4]Pierre Teilhard De Chardin, *Christianity and Evolution*, Harcourt Brace Jovanovich, Inc., N.Y., 1969.

[5]Ann Belford Ulanov, *The Feminine in Jungian Psychology and in Christian Theology*, Northwestern U. Press, Evanston, 1972, p. 155.

[6]R.P. McBrien, *Catholicism*, Winston Press, Minneapolis, Mn., 1980, pp. 777–783.

3

THE SOIL IN WHICH WE MUST GROW

A key attribute of the higher levels of consciousness is the striving for more constructive relationships with others. This has to be done in the real world of evil, sin, and suffering. We need to accept that reality and still find our fulfillment. Somehow, in the midst of this, we need to develop a sense of community that is helpful to all. An extension of this is the question of the further reality of a guiding force, that we call God, and how our fulfillment is related to that. The soil in which we must grow is this entire universe, - the space and time of the suffering world and also the hypothesized other reality we associate with a Divine Providence.

3.1 THE HYPOTHESIS OF GOD

Cause and Effect

Relating the ideal of full personhood to the evolution of consciousness, which we elaborated on above, sounds rational to us; but we realize that it leads to another question. Is there really a direction to all this evolution, towards increasing complexity and consciousness? If so, what is the cause of this direction, and will it remain?

29

Or is it only a transient phenomena, even an illusion? Are we just whistling bravely in the dark of a meaningless, unguided, chance creation? Our need for a sense of purpose and value demands some answers.

Is all in this life absurd, without purpose or meaning? Is the entire process, over billions of years, to end in nothing, under the relentless pressure of forces of dissipation? We are inherently creatures of hope. Can we rationally put our hope in a force that urges a positive direction towards greater complexity and consciousness (as we think has been observed)? If so, what is the nature of that force?

Any hypothesis about the purpose and meaning of life frequently comes up against this question of cause. Perhaps, we venture, there is no cause! Then, we fall back to the argument that pure chance has resulted in this phenomenal order and beauty, - in the human body, in the world of nature in general. Mathematical calculations would seem to give a high probability to chaos and disorder, as any gambler will tell you, if all were purely random. Natural selection (survival of the fittest) certainly plays a role. But, to us, this also seems insufficient, in itself, to explain the marvelous ability to enjoy a concert, appreciate a sunset, and sacrifice for others. Perhaps something more must be at work, to carry the evolution through to these wonderful results. Furthermore, there's heavy evidence that dissipation, degeneration, and chaos are constant threats. One only has to recall the horrors of the holocaust, the violence in our cities, or the nuclear threat, to remember that any positive direction is far from a natural certainty. In particular, man apparently has the freedom to completely reverse any positive direction. Sometimes it seems that we enjoy too much living at the animal level. Yet, there is, over the centuries, an unsteady drift to higher complexity; and it is yet possible that this unsteady drift to higher consciousness will prevail! On the one hand, the explanation of the universe as a random, chance occurrence, seems highly improbable to a great many who have puzzled about this. On the other hand, all of the results are not yet in, and there is no certainty that a positive direction will be maintained.

The human's inquiring mind naturally seeks to understand in wider and wider dimensions. We explore all of space and time with our mind's eye. A quantum leap, consistent with that urge to search, is to contemplate the possibilities of a reality beyond our senses, and of a direction-setting force, a divinity of some kind, with which we may be somehow associated.

The keystone hypothesis, then, is the existence of that force which draws the universe towards greater complexity and consciousness. That hypothesis fits the observed data of steadily increasing consciousness which we find in creation. If there is a source for this direction-setting force, then that entity, by deduction, is characterized by higher levels of complexity and consciousness, beyond anything we now experience. For many, this source of the direction-setting force is associated with a concept called God.

A Limited View

We benefit a great deal from the inspiration, tradition, and dogma of those who went before us. We'll examine some of that later in Chapter 6. First, however, let's continue to approach the issue of God, as a plausible hypothesis. As with every subject that we try to understand and express, our hypothesis can be made more concrete with models and symbols which express our concepts. The ultimate reality is, in this case, beyond us. Our understanding is necessarily limited, incomplete, bounded by our own finite intellect and our own narrow culture. Our models and symbols are, accordingly, bound to be similarly deficient. Nevertheless, we know from experience that even such deficient models can be most useful in explaining parts of the mystery and in effectively guiding our actions in many real situations.

Hence, we may accept the hypothesis of the existence of God and desire to acquire as good a model of this indistinct reality as we can. At the same time, we should be aware of the probable limitations of both our understanding and the models we eagerly use. We'll never be able to achieve a perfect model. Our understanding is limited by the reality we can perceive; and this limits our concepts of an ultimate source of consciousness and an ultimate destination for the evolution of creation.

In our daily lives, consciousness is roughly characterized by parameters called empathy, caring love, and kindness. The ultimate consciousness, therefore, is likewise described by these parameters. We crudely say, "God is love." This may be only a rough symbol, an incomplete model, but it may serve us well as a first approximate concept. We need not presume that such is a complete description or the only or best description. We use these simple models even though we recognize that God's attributes probably exceed ours beyond our comprehension. Moreover, what we first sense as a vast difference in degree (of qualities like love), probably phases into a difference in kind,[1] which humans cannot understand.

Corollaries

We observe the 'phenomenon of man' and the world of nature further, and try to fill in more of our model. A corollary concept, again consistent with the reality we perceive, is that all of God's creation seems to share in some way these parameters of creativity and consciousness. Particularly in this more recent creation, the human being, there is evident a high potential for both of these parameters. A further consistent corollary is that the Divine Providence has set in motion the process which could create a harmonious unity of the created with the creator. We each experience it somewhat. Deep within us is the spark of the will to live, and to live more fully. Many people, down through the ages, have observed that eventually this inner spark is dissatisfied with the usual pursuits of pleasure and success. The selfish aspects of wealth, fame, and power begin to leave a poor taste. Our inner spirit, an inner force, moves us to grow towards some higher ideal, which may at first include duty, social dedication and similar activities proceeding from a fuller consciousness. Finally, the human spirit longs for a good that is infinite and eternal. Thus, we are part of an evolutionary process, wherein our consciousness grows. This, apparently, is in harmony with a direction-setting force, that can be characterized by an ultimate consciousness.

A logical extension would seem to be that each person is created with the potential of becoming, to some degree, an 'image and likeness' of God. Further, this potential calls for the presence, in each person, of some seed, as it were, of the Divine Providence. This common understanding is often expressed by phrases like "God be with you," or "The spirit of God was in her," or "He was born again of the spirit," or "There is something of God in every human being." That seed, we suggest, urges us towards greater consciousness, - that is, towards greater awareness of others, and of a Divine 'other', and of ourselves in relation to these. We are urged to build that relationship in empathy and caring love, and hence to practice kindness at every opportunity.

A corresponding concept is that we each have a creative role and a birthing role, in the building of consciousness both in ourselves and in others. Every constructive action that we take contributes a ripple of goodness that propagates in the world, and affects those who encounter it. We thus enable the acceptance of the Spirit of God by others, and these effects also have a life of their own, affecting still others, and so on. This leads to the concept of the 'birth of God', as a continuous process, and the role that we each play in that.

Meister Eckhart puts it in a startling metaphor, saying that "Everyone will be the mother of God."[2] Understanding this requires that we each see ourselves as an integral part of God's creation and of his plan, which includes growth in consciousness; each of us can be a birthing mechanism for the fulfillment of God's plan. What a role, indeed!

Multiple Sources

The relation of the theory of God to the concept of consciousness is found in many places and in different forms. We all experience an urging towards enlightenment and full personhood. The Quakers, for example, refer to this inspiration by the term 'inner light', which is quite expressive. It connotes a seeing of a broader view, in a better light. For them, this inner light is an actuality and an essential part of a person's being. Many cultures over many ages have sensed something similar. Hindus seek to exercise and control the mind so as to make contact with the reservoir of being that underlies and animates our personality, with a component of our being that never dies, is never exhausted, and is without limit in awareness and bliss.[3] Buddhists believe we work in stages towards an enlightenment that dissolves the boundaries between ourselves and others.[4] Teilhard de Chardin sees humanity moving imperceptibly but surely towards that state of higher consciousness that approaches unity with God, which is the ultimate consciousness.[5]

The Bible, too, is full of perceptions of God as the friend, lover, and giver, who wants us to work towards an ultimate fulfillment in harmony with others. The future dream he has for us is expressed, for example, in Isaiah 11:6-9 in the prophecy of the wolf living with the lamb. The dream is that we should grow in consciousness, give of ourselves for our neighbor, and treat those around us with love and concern, so then we might be able to rest with our former enemies, and walk in dangerous places unharmed. The New Testament further emphasizes the concepts of a providential, forgiving, and encouraging God, as in Jesus' approach to 'abba', the loving father. This, it seems to us, best meets the tests of life experiences, despite the problems of suffering, which we'll discuss later.

One cannot absolutely prove the existence of God; nor can one prove that God does not exist. However, the hypothesis of the existence of a providential, consciousness-fostering God, drawn from many sources, is, it seems to us, consistent with the observed phenomenon of humankind, with the essence of personhood as we see it, and with the evolutionary concepts that we are yet growing and becoming.

The models we put together to describe God are bound to be very approximate, from a particular vantage point, and not the only useful model. However, the adherence to the hypothesis of God's existence is not illogical; it is consistent, in the long run, with the observed facts; and it can be very constructive and productive. Like the hypotheses in physics, its corollaries can be designed to match observed phenomena, and then its use yields good results that improve our productivity. It can be a strong contribution to 'making the person', as it helps to give direction, meaning, and purpose to our lives.

We, the writers, like most of humankind, do accept this hypothesis, of a providential, direction-setting force, that we call God; and through this acceptance we find that our lives are greatly altered. The ideal of consciousness, in space and time, is expanded. Our added consciousness of the existence and presence of a providential God provides a stability to the hypothesis of consciousness evolution. We then can, with greater confidence, dedicate and commit ourselves to the fulfillment of that evolution of consciousness. We each are thus small co-creators in partnership with God. We acquire greater confidence in the purpose and meaning of our existence. Life is worth living! Would you not agree that any hypothesis which does all that, is well worth considering?

3.2 FREE WILL AND THE EXISTENCE OF EVIL

The Ability To Choose

We claim that there's an inner urge to survive and to grow. However, the acceptance of this potential to grow and the pursuit of this potential still, obviously, depend on us, as free persons. Humans evidently can choose, in many instances, between actions that move them up or down, - that is, either in a direction that maximizes love or in a direction that does not do so, or even directly contributes to dissipation.

Some, on the other hand, would deny that people truly have free will. They would argue that we are 'programmed' in many ways. Our environment sets our outlook. Our surrounding culture colors our views. We are brain-washed from infancy to accept some things and reject others. Our economic pressures force us to certain actions, and so forth. One cannot deny that there is some truth in all this, for the effects are apparent. But does that take away man's free will, and if so, to what extent?

Humans apparently also have this unique capability to step aside, as it were, and view themselves. If we are programmed, then, strangely, we can know that we are. But with that knowledge, one is in a position to combat the programming! Everyday, in fact, one must choose among many alternatives, some of which are, in fact, things we've learned, were told, or which were otherwise 'programmed' into us. Yes, it seems that we certainly are 'programmed', to some degree; but there remains sufficient detachment to enable us (often with great difficulty) to exercise that most precious ability to choose whether or not to follow the program!

In a real sense, we find that this choosing also continuously shapes our personhood, both now and for the future. Thus, as is often said, we are not finished; we are still becoming; and we each have a part to play in our own continuing creation! Every decision we make contributes in a small way to our pattern of thinking. It therefore modifies the automatic tendencies for future behavior. In effect it contributes, at least slightly, to a new 'program' that we will be inclined to follow later on. Thus we create ourselves, bit by bit. Though these patterns may fade away, a residue can remain for a long time, - sometimes, apparently, even for life. If this is true, perhaps we'd better be conscious of the fact that we never live 'just for the moment', but always are in process of creating for the future. Then, only by future conscious decisions, sometimes with great effort, can we depart from that earlier created program. Happily, that departure then becomes another major step in our development. We keep getting another chance.

Accepting the reality of free will, within the above limits, implies an acceptance of responsibility for our actions. This can be uncomfortable. No longer can one blame entirely one's mother, father, associates, poverty, or culture. These are surely factors that influence us; but the bottom line seems to be the fact that each person has the inherent capacity to steer the directions for his or her actions, and is therefore responsible for the consequences.

We realize further that this role of ours in creation can be a planned role. Like an author of a novel or a director of a play, we have the ability to create a mental image of the person we want to become. This is naturally a continuing process, with the image of our 'ideal' evolving as we mature. Creating a realistic, achievable, desirable image does take decision and work. Then, the more clearly and vividly we make that image, the more it becomes a part of us. We can, if we wish, keep that image in mind and increasingly shape our attitudes and actions to be in harmony with that projection.

Our free will can be exercised in stages: First we can choose among what some call our 'fundamental options', to set our general course. This may be a conscious set of decisions or it may be only a careless acceptance of a general course. An example of a fundamental option would be to have concern for one's neighbor. Next, we are forced to make choices in specific situations, and these can be made in the light of our earlier choices of fundamental options. Thus, by our decisions, we continually contribute to our own creation, becoming more or less a complete person.

We greatly value this freedom to choose what we believe to be 'good'. We sometimes need to choose a path different from the majority; and sometimes we even need to choose civil disobedience, against what we believe to be unjust laws. People fight and die to preserve the right of honest dissent. They are often willing to suffer any consequences, if necessary.

And yet there is often disagreement as to whether, in certain matters, we should have 'free choice' or not. How can this be? Part of the answer is, again, the different spheres of space or time over which different people make their decisions. For me alone, I may choose to maximize the apparent good to me today; however, that may at the same time hurt another, or it may cause someone grief later on. Hence, we have proponents and opponents of 'free choice' in different matters. Ginny Desmond Billinger, a Minnesota feminist, illustrates this by saying that she is anti-choice on spouse beating, child abuse, drunken driving, abortion, handgun ownership, whale hunting, seal clubbing, and dumping hazardous wastes. She says that "the road to freedom cannot be paved with the sacrificed rights of others."[6] On the other hand, one can find vocal persons who will insist that each of these examples is a private matter for them to decide alone. The different spheres of consciousness help to make the difference in judgement. It's well, therefore, to ask which side, in any argument, is taking the broader view in space and time.

This freedom to choose, then, has a role to play in both our own development and the evolutionary development of the world in which we live. Jay Mc Daniel puts it this way:

> God's creativity ... is that of a continuous and ongoing process that potentially draws the universe into new forms of actuality relative to what is possible in each situation. The very efficacy of this creativity depends on the creative response of the actualities that are drawn. In their freedom, they may or may not respond to the divine lure. This means that at any given moment what is happening in the universe is not the result of God's creativity alone, or of the universe's alone, but rather the result of the joint creativity of God and the universe.[7]

Thus, we have the opportunity to be creative partners in the greatest undertaking imaginable.

Evil

We say that each choice has some potential for good or evil; but still, we might ask, what is evil? Too often we assume a simplistic duality of good and evil, of God versus the devil. A more rational starting point, we think, is that evil might be defined as anything that obstructs or reduces humankind's fulfillment of it's true destiny. If, as we've hypothesized, that destiny is to grow in consciousness, - for example, in empathy, caring love, and kindness, then evil is that which reduces this. Every day, in countless ways, we choose between greater or less consciousness. In making our judgements, and choosing our course, we intuitively consider our relationships and responsibilities towards ourselves, the world, other people, and God. We either strive, with all of our being, to maximize the good, in all the space and time we can comprehend, or we do something less than that. That something less is, to some degree, less good. Hence, should this be termed evil?

That may be a pretty basic and realistic way to define evil, rather than only by some set of rules and laws. It's also consistent with experience, where the hard decisions are often not between something that is clearly good and something that is clearly evil. It often is a decision between something good and something better, or an attempt to choose the lesser of two evils. Sometimes, too, we need to constrain one good in order to gain full advantage of another good; or we may have to constrain one good now in order to obtain a greater good later on. Maximizing the good thus involves stretching our consciousness of the alternatives and the consequences of each action on others both now and later. As Hans Kung explains, God's plan is man's fulfillment.[8] We would add that fulfillment of humankind comes from the development and exercise of consciousness in broad space and time; and evil is what impedes or detracts from that plan of God.

On the other hand, in daily life, we often can't see the full spectrum of alternatives. Our view is usually narrowed to the local scene and a few options. We may then be tempted to choose a morally dubious alternative, in the interests of what we believe to be a greater good. The experiences of the My Lai massacre in Vietnam, the fire-bombing of the city of Dresden in World War II, and many crimes in our cities, have been excused by such rationalizations. To guard against such narrowed vision, society sets standareds, ethics, and laws, which in effect say that certain acts are intolerable under any circumstances. Churches, similarly, identify those acts which appear to them to be inherently evil, as viewed in the broad perspective of God's plan for humanity.

Of course, our ordinary free-will decisions can also reduce the overall good, and thus promote evil. For example, we can submit to our laziness or otherwise allow a lowering of our expectations of ourselves and of others. We can choose to act with less empathy, caring love, and kindness than that of which we are capable. We can neglect to act responsibly. Even negative emotions, such as anger and fear, involve some kind of permission. Thus, we can often fail to seize the opportunity to contribute to our increasing consciousness.

Quite a different class of evils includes those which provide physical obstacles to the fulfillment of humanity, such as disease, hunger, and natural disasters. This is a reflection of our living in an imperfect world. These environmental evils undoubtedly cause great anguish and can impede the growth of consciousness. However, it is not certain that they, in themselves, must always reduce consciousness in the long run. The individuals in the disaster situation may be creating more loving consciousness than the more fortunate ones who are under less stress. For example, we've seen the tremendous outpouring of compassion and assistance in the great earthquake at Mexico City, in 1985. It is more certain that evil is increased by failure to exercise our potential for consciousness. Too often we are reluctant to focus human energy, so as to ameliorate such conditions and to help others recover from such disasters.

Other external obstacles to fulfillment are the many forms of injustice and oppression, which dehumanize persons and restrict freedom, as seems evident in the most depressed societies. We feel particular anguish in these social evils as we see many of them originating in the misguided decisions of other human beings.

Actually, what we discern as good and evil must be greatly influenced by our frame of reference, - namely, our culture. What God sees, therefore, may be quite different. Since all has been created by God, and all is within God's providence, all may be more a part of God's plan than we realize. In this perspective, one is hard-pressed to find anything that cannot have a place in God's intended process. We might hypothesize that all things might be more a matter of different degrees of progress in the evolutionary plan. Then, even evil has its place, perhaps because its possibility gives the human, through his freedom to make choices, the opportunity to grow.

A similar view holds that the world which God made is truly good; and what we call evil are the lesser choices, the poorer choices, the choices that detract from empathy, caring love and kindness; and all these become the opportunity for further creative development. Jay McDaniel reflects Eastern theological views when he says, further, "As events in the world transpire, God becomes aware of them, and they become part of God. The divine aims are themselves adjusted for subsequent events in accordance with what has happened."[9] If our purpose here is to manufacture love, then all of the poor choices become the soil and fertilizer from which we produce love. Thus, the poor criminal justice system in the U.S. is not so much an evil but a system that needs perfecting through our efforts. Even abortion might be seen in that light. Abortion, perhaps, is a social condition that makes society ponder and pull together the ideas of what is loving, what is selfish, what enhances the total quality of life, and how we maximize the total good in space and time.

Although apparently undesirable, it seems that what we have called evil is essential to the exercise of our precious gift of freedom to choose and to create good. If that option were not present, we might truly be automatons, programmed to do the maximum good, without any choice in the matter. Would not this be totally inconsistent with the achievement of personal fulfillment? Perhaps only with the options for evil do we have the opportunity to achieve our destiny to creatively grow towards full consciousness.

The Right Path?

But just what choices yield the maximum good in a given situation? Other persons' choices will undoubtedly be somewhat different from ours. Who is right? Again, we have to admit that our knowledge is limited, our view is culturally distorted, and our judgment is overly influenced by local awareness, rather than a broader awareness in space and time. We are each, therefore, bound to make different judgements; and each is bound to be, to some degree, 'wrong'. Our role, nevertheless can only be to seek the best guidance we can find; to make the best decisions we are capable of, at the moment; to recognize the imperfection of every step; and to constantly seek those 'mid-course-corrections' which will redirect us towards our goal of maximizing consciousness.

In this, we accept our responsibility to do our best to assess what is good and what is evil. We each have a role to play, so we each must make decisions. Persons, groups, and institutions do in fact act at times as forces that promote evil. It's a great disservice not to recognize this, or to be tolerant of it. What is clearly evil to us (even if we are mistaken in our judgement) must always be opposed. How is such opposition consistent with consciousness? The trick is to forcefully oppose evil, but nevertheless to respect the persons involved. If another person is involved, as an opponent, one must still respect the inherent potential for full personhood that is in the opponent. While necessarily opposing him, one must, hopefully, try to aid the growth of the opponent or to transform the situation, without resorting to means which in themselves are evil or promote evil.

Thus, it's evident that our free-will is a most precious asset. With it, despite pressures, we set ourselves apart from our internal 'programs'. By our countless decisions we contribute to our own creation, following an ideal we envision. Gladly taking up the challenge and the opportunity, we all maximize the 'good' in space and time, as best we can perceive it; and we constantly redirect our path as we see this 'good' more clearly.

3.3 THE ADULT EXECUTIVE

Another interesting model, or way of describing the human being, is in terms of three major components of self.[10] These are the Child, or the impulses springing from our lower levels of consciousness; the Parent, representing all that we have learned or been taught; and finally the Adult, representing those higher levels of consciousness that strive to provide an overall harmony within the entire self. We are inclined, at times, to function somewhat automatically, following the Child or the Parent. The Adult in us, however, is needed to assert our full personhood and take full responsibility for ourselves. It is this assertion, through use of our highest levels of consciousness, that builds the full person and makes life worth living.

We may happily follow our childish impulses, react instinctively, and simply live for 'what feels good' to us at the moment. Sometimes that is the best possible course, for play can be very healthy and constructive. Simply following the Child in us, however, may not be best. It may be far better to steer that energy into other channels. For example, when we feel that we are being opposed by another, our anger may begin to rise, and we may simply follow that impulse and explode, to 'show him'. On the other hand, a little consideration of the underlying needs of the opponent might reveal a different story. Alternative approaches could be considered. The opponent might then prove to be malleable and come closer to our view. Perhaps a more mild expression of concern would in the long run bring us greater rewards. That would be the Adult (and broader consciousness) at work, using the human attributes of empathy, imagination, and creativity. On the other hand, we may somewhat blindly follow the patterns of our culture. After all, what has been taught to us by parents, and by institutions, and by people around us, has been extremely valuable and important to us. These sources of knowledge have fed us and guided us for many years; and we are usually loathe to entertain thoughts of their deficiencies or weaknesses. To do so seems to take away our anchor and leave us somewhat adrift.

However, history is full of examples where culturally acceptable practices have later on proven to be inappropriate or even
abhorrent. What is right, proper, and good for the local time, may
become inappropriate as time passes and circumstances change.
Slavery and all forms of discrimination are commonplace examples of such socially accepted abhorrent and intolerant practices.
Even today, apartheid is justified in the minds of many South
Africans; it has become an integral part of the culture for many,
though it is seen as archaic by most thinking people. The Adult in
us can step aside and assess even our culture, and decide,
personally, whether the culture is appropriate today or not.

Thus, we have a higher level of consciousness that can accept
or reject the impulses of either the 'Child' in us or the effects of a
'Parent' in us. How we develop and use that 'Adult' ability largely
determines what kind of person we become.

To make the point by stretching it, the human robot, following established 'programs', and the contented slave have a
great deal of certainty and stability in their lives. Simply following
is sufficient for them. However, that is not the full potential of the
person God created; it is not what each person can become. The
process of becoming that full person requires the exercise of those
higher levels of consciousness, - to assess our lower-level childish
impulses, and also to assess the teachings of our culture. We can
and therefore must continually establish our own reference
points, reformulate our own ideals, and in that light, assess the
recommendations of our Child and our Parent. Then, we must
decide as best we can on our individual course of action. In many
cases, this can be done imaginatively, and the creative, even
artistic aspects of such action gives zest and pleasure to living.

3.4 USING SUFFERING

Sooner or later we have to face the fact that humankind suffers a
great deal. In addition to natural disasters and disease, there are
the man-made sufferings caused by oppression and injustice.
Moreover, there is an inequity; some suffer more than others. The
logic, purpose, or justice of all of this is indeed hard to understand, and perhaps it is simply beyond us.

One can speculate that pain, suffering, and evil must be
within God's providence, as well as goodness and kindness. Even

as God is a part of all goodness, so, too, he must partake of all suffering. Obviously, however, God's existence, if he exists at all, must be both with humankind and vastly beyond it. On the one hand, a truly all-loving God must experience some form of compassion for the suffering ones that are loved. On the other hand, it's also reasonable to expect that God is not tortured by suffering the way humankind is, because God may see all suffering as an ultimate benefit to humankind, within a vastly larger scope of reality than we see it. Even now, we gladly suffer at times to achieve a higher purpose. The pains of childbirth do not deter most women from wanting and having children, for example.

In addition, we begin to perceive that each person is in some sense a part of God, and that we too may have some sort of existence with God beyond this life. In that broader view, suffering in this life is only part of a process leading to greater value beyond the suffering. In that view, we see the beauty of all creation, the bountiful nature of this world, and particularly the marvelous gift of ourselves. All this leads us to see God as a loving and gracious provider, in whom we can trust (Job 38-41). Thus our awareness of God and our trust in him tends to give hope for an end to suffering and to make interim suffering more bearable.

The example given by Jesus, regarding suffering, is likewise thought provoking. He did not shirk it, but accepted it as part of his mission and part of his purpose, presumably to a greater end result. His continuation beyond death is a powerful suggestion that the passage through suffering is not without purpose, and that the hope of passage and what lies beyond can sustain us. Thus, Hans Kung says:

> By following this Jesus, even in the world of today, man is able not only to act but to suffer, not only to live but to die, in a truly human way. And even when 'pure reason' breaks down, even in pointless misery and sin, he perceives a meaning; for he knows that here, too, in both positive and negative experience, he is sustained by God. This faith in Jesus the Christ gives peace with God and with oneself, but does not play down the problems of the world and society.[11]

Recall, also, how we have compassion for those who suffer. In effect, suffering generates empathy and compassion in others. If, as we believe, humankind is evolving to higher levels of consciousness, then might not this generation of compassion have a contribution to that evolution? If we recall our own suffering, and the effects of it, or even if we only have compassion for those who suffer, doesn't it seem that our awareness also broadens to better understand the needs of others? The experience of our pain helps us to understand and somehow helps us to experience the pain of others. Bonhoeffer expressed it in prison this way:

> There remains an experience of incomparable value. We have for once learned to see the great events of the world from below, from the perspective of the outcast, the suspects, the maltreated, the powerless, the oppressed, the reviled - in short, from the perspective of those who suffer. ...We have to learn that personal suffering is a more effective key, a more rewarding principle for exploring the world in thought and action than personal good fortune.[12]

One close-to-home example of that, we think, is a friend of ours who has had such anguish over a beautiful daughter turned drug addict and alcoholic. There are few heart-rending events to compare with such self destruction of a loved one over a long period. And yet, our friend is able to reach deep for strength and hope; and more than that, we see the products of that expressed in very deep compassion for the handicapped and the imprisoned.

When that suffering is freely undertaken for the good of others, then, it's clear that empathy, caring love, and kindness can be involved. One would feel that the evolution of humankind towards full consciousness is somehow enhanced. But what if suffering is imposed on one without his consent? Even then, many suggest that one can at least offer that suffering to God, in the hope that this expenditure will somehow be to the benefit of others. That philosophy is part of the notion that we have bonds of consciousness with the Divine Providence, and hence with all persons of good will. This assignment of purpose to suffering, offering it up to God for others, is itself an act of consciousness. One might expect that it, too, contributes to the 'world-economy' in consciousness. At the same time, it evidently brings a sense of peace to the sufferer that is otherwise difficult to achieve.

Our suffering has another interesting side effect. Too often, we're entranced by the glitter of some selfish or otherwise narrow pursuit. False, transient pleasures are often large in our lives. A period of suffering, however, has a remarkable way of dissipating all that confusion. Often after the period of suffering, we're much clearer on what is really important and worthwhile.

Of course there are many kinds of suffering: physical, mental, and psychological. There's even a suffering when we are subject to erroneous or harmful cultures or religious concepts. One suffers from the harm that poor ideas can do to us; we suffer again as we struggle to oppose the status quo. Is it also possible that such errors in philosophy and religion could likewise be beneficial? Here, too, it takes great strength of character to find one's way, - indeed to fight one's way out of the 'conventional wisdom' to a better view. Perhaps again, only by the struggle to clarify or correct can we really mature and progress.

Different persons, of course, have a different ability to cope with suffering. In part, this seems to depend on their breadth of vision. God didn't promise that our lives would be all sunshine and no rain. He did, however, give us the capability to remain trusting, hopeful, and even cheerful in the midst of pain. We all find it difficult to really live this philosophy. It often takes much time and patient trust in God's wisdom before these thoughts can be fully accepted.

3.5 HEALING WITH FORGIVENESS

We believe that another prime characteristic of the fulfilled person is the inclination to forgive; so let's observe how forgiveness seems to work and what it means.

What Is Forgiveness?

We all like to be forgiven; however, we often find it difficult to forgive. When we are wronged, there is a tendency to seek revenge. There is a cleavage between the two parties, so the wronged party often does not include the other party in its sphere for maximizing the good. One can readily sympathize with this, particularly when a strong defense mechanism is involved. We feel that we must protect ourselves from the 'aggressor'; and offense is often the best defense. But is this again only the residue of that earlier instinct for brute survival? Where, then, does forgiveness come in? To take a concrete example, when you are assailed on the street, by a man with a knife, do you 'turn the other cheek', or do you fight? Do you forgive? What does it really mean, to forgive, in real life?

Let's look at this in the light of the ideal to maximize consciousness. If we are to be faithful to our ideal, we must, in every situation, strive to enlarge the sphere in which we seek to maximize the total good. In particular, that must include our assailant, as well as ourselves. However, the well-being that we desire for him must be exactly that which makes him a full person, his growth to full consciousness. The defensive action we take, then, in the short-term, is not necessarily inconsistent with a desire for his longer-term growth. Instead of revenge, and a desire for destruction, we can defend ourselves with the minimum violence needed. That minimized violence can be genuinely accompanied by a desire for correction of the other and subsequent movement towards ultimate growth, as well as our own preservation.

Forgiveness, then, can perhaps be defined as the desire for the other's well-being and his continued growth in personhood, despite the past offense. It is the opposite of seeking revenge and destruction. Forgiveness is accompanied by the freedom of the forgiver from the corrosion of hate or self-pity. The forgiver returns to the path of full personhood (including compassion for the aggressor), and is exhilarated by it. The considerate response adds to one's own sense of self-worth. It heals both parties, and so permits renewed growth. But all this is not inconsistent with forceful but careful defense, which may be necessary to maximize the total good, as one sees it at the moment.

With this understanding, we are inclined not to condemn the 'aggressor', but instead to want his ultimate growth, if that is possible, while resisting the aggression. Nevertheless, we are right, it seems, in denouncing the 'aggression' as a failure. (Often it seems to involve a failure to seek fulfillment at a higher level, and to be content with a delusion of fulfillment at a lower level.)

Perhaps the most unique aspect of Jesus' teaching was his emphasis on forgiveness "not seven but seventy times seven times" (Matthew 18:22) - that is, without limit. Yet he was not in any way content with failure. When Jesus spoke to the woman taken in adultery, he said, "Go and sin no more". He realized that continuing as she was would not be for her true fulfillment. Also, when Jesus was struck on the face, while standing before the high priest, he did not simply 'turn the other cheek'. Instead, he emphasized the relationship between himself and the aggressor by asking, "If there is something wrong in what I said, point it out; but if there is no offense in it, why do you strike me?" (John 18:23) So forgiveness is not permissiveness. In fact, if a person has flagrantly committed acts that society sees as reprehensible, society can show its displeasure and its forgiveness by both confining that person in prison and by actively facilitating his rehabilitation. We must renounce each failure to move on to a higher consciousness, and then strive to find ways to encourage each person to so move.

Forgiving is not being a 'door-mat', letting people enjoy walking all over you. On the other hand, it is not slamming the door on the other, either. It is somewhere in between these extremes. It is like opening the door somewhat, and seeking the way to cooperate in the other's ultimate renewal. It is a beginning and not a completion; it is setting the direction towards cooperation. Forgiveness is thus not passive; it must be accompanied by some action, direct or indirect, which is aimed at improving the situation which caused the offense.

Forgiveness often involves 'letting go' of bitterness towards, or hatred of, others who have hurt us. That 'letting go' is a freeing action. We 'let go', for example, when we laugh; we 'let go' of our anxieties when we relax ourselves for sleep after an exhausting day; we 'let go' of our crippling guilt when we forgive ourselves in the light of God's hope for us. But perhaps the greater freedom comes for some when they 'let go' of the resentment they carry around, which distorts their lives. Doing that can be extremely difficult; it often takes time to accomplish. Freedom finally comes when they decide to set this constraint and corrosion of their lives aside, - when they decide to forgive so that they can enjoy the experiences of healing others, love more fully, and live more fully.

Forgiving Ourselves

It follows that, when we have erred, we should expect others of good will to forgive us. We should seek forgiveness, first for the hurt we have caused anyone, and second for the harm we may have done to the environment or the culture, which in turn may hurt someone. Above all, we need to forgive ourselves, and expect to be forgiven by an all-loving God.

However, self-forgiveness is not always easy; and it can be blocked by a myopic sense of guilt. When our vision is limited to ourselves, and we focus primarily on our difficulties, we may be

unable to truly forgive ourselves. This can easily become agoniz-
ing, and in some desperation, we may seek almost any way to get
rid of the guilt. Sometimes, this leads us to blame someone else.
We often seem to want to think that our inadequacies are
somehow the fault of others. Considering 'them' to be outside the
sphere of our optimization of good, we may separate ourselves
from them, or even attack them. As in so many other examples,
we see a contraction of the spheres of consciousness. A person in
this state may attack anyone, in an irrational belief that 'they' are
somehow responsible for his failures. Hurting the others may give
momentary satisfaction, but it's sure to later result in a greater
burden of guilt.

It often seems that problems of this sort start with an
exaggerated sense of guilt, caused by too narrow a view. We
ourselves, and not anyone else, may be responsible for creating
that original sense of failure, inadequacy, and self-rejection.
Certainly, we need to learn from our bitter experiences; certainly,
we need to strive ever more to direct ourselves to where we can
achieve greater fulfillment; but despite all failures, if we broaden
our consciousness, we will find that we are still beloved sons or
daughters of God. God's love makes all inadequacies and all
failures relatively inconsequential.

Divine forgiveness looks to our ultimate fulfillment despite
any and all setbacks. Recognition of divine love can set us free of
the chains that may bind us, - any sense of inferiority, guilt, or fear.
In communion with our loving and forgiving God, we are free.
Moreover, since God works through people, each one of us can be
the channel of God's love; hence each one of us, by our love of
others, can also set others free.

We can try to retain a consciousness of ourselves and others
as the common recipients of that love of God. With that consciousness, we can see that we and others are still potentially beautiful
children of God. We can alter recollections of hurt we've suffered
to include the fact that a loving God was present even in those
difficult situations. We can try to understand that a loving God
was still looking forward to the recovery of our opponents, at the
very moment of their aggression. In that light, we can forgive
others for their inadequacies; and then, perhaps, it is easier to
similarly forgive ourselves. Hopefully, we can thus avoid destructive images of guilt, and then get on with living more fully.

A sobering conclusion is that, given the imperfections of the
world, - ourselves and all those around us, the pursuit of the ideal,

to maximize consciousness, must involve an active sense of forgiveness, of others and of ourselves. The good news is that we can forgive; we can respond to the urgings of that spark of a forgiving God within us. We can free ourselves; and as we do, we find that the more we forgive, the more we ourselves grow and find greater fulfillment.

3.6 THE BONDS OF COMMUNITY

Who are the ones who seem to get the most out of life? Isn't it true that these people do not live in isolation, but rather live as cooperating elements in loving communities?

The Nature of Communities

One can find a vast hierarchy of cooperating elements, all along the evolutionary path. The cooperation among particles can be observed within the most basic elements. The cooperation among dissimilar elements becomes even more evident in macro molecules, and living cells. Everyone is also familiar with the organization of cooperative roles in the ant colonies and bee-hives. At some point in this evolutionary process, the human species appeared. As expressed in the Bible, God said, "Let us make humankind in our image!" He made men and women, diverse, and wonderful, and able to understand and cooperate in still more profound ways.

This cooperation in communities, then, is in the very nature of all creation. In all this diversity, the religious person sees a unity in God's unfolding creation. God is evidenced in all the expressions of beauty that he created. The complexity and cooperation of the molecules reveals him, as does the sun sparkling through iced trees on a wintry morning. His is the intelligence of humankind, and of the lion stalking majestically through a green jungle. In each, there are different levels of complexity, consciousness, and evidence of evolving community.

The message of the Bible also seems to be that God had a dream for us, a dream that we would be much like God, in some way. Adam and Eve are presented as the example of a loving community. They were made for each other, to be helpmates, to be friends. They are two different creatures; but in the Bible story,

God saw their great possibilities as a community of love. Human
beings were given the potential for inter-relationships at higher
levels than was possible in other parts of the creation. Human
communities could foster unity while retaining individual
freedom and creativity.

We are each in this process that evolves higher levels of
community. Still, it seems that we need to make an effort to be a
fully functioning part of a true community. All of us are crying out
for genuine, mutual, friendship; nevertheless, we seem too often
to build barriers that tend to smother that cry. We are all, in our
search for friendship, in need of reaching out. But, often, we don't
realize this; then, instead of attracting friendship by seeking
directly to be truly human, in empathy, caring love, and kindness,
we may try to be superior. We may try to get admiration by
enhancing our power over others, or by our supposedly superior
intelligence, or simply by our financial success. Haven't we all
found that this doesn't work? We finally realize that we must seek
to be fully human, and that we must accept the truth of our need
for mutual friendship and love. Then we have a better chance to
experience true contentment.

Participation in a community, however, always exposes us to
some degree. Whether we admit it or not, we are each vulnerable
to every person with whom we have contact. Fortunately, most
participation in community does not involve vulnerability to
physical harm. There is, instead, vulnerability to rejection and
perhaps frustration or disappointment. We may even feel vulnerable to abuse and devoid of our accustomed protection. We can
admit and accept our vulnerability, and yet refuse to let that stop
us; then we will be better able to enter into community with each
other.

Occasionally, one may be asked to to be seriously exposed for
the benefit of the community or one of its members. Do you
remember the story of Kitty Genovese? She was suddenly and
brutally attacked in New York City by a mindless knife wielder.
Repeatedly, he attacked, and was frightened away by her
screams. And repeatedly he returned to stab her again, when no
one came to help. The police later estimated that about fifty people
in nearby apartments heard, watched, listened, waited, and did
nothing. Is it too strong to say that Kitty Genovese was murdered
by up to fifty persons, one of whom used a knife? The others may
have facilitated the killing by their earlier rejections of calls to a
sense of community.

We all see too many people sit on the sidelines. Community

doesn't happen to a person 'out of the blue sky'; comradeship of others and the respect of others in the community doesn't come to a person who just waits for that to happen. Rather, the person must decide to act for the benefit of community; the person has to reach out, establish contact with others, and contribute to the community. Only then will that person enjoy the fruits of community.

The group achievement is greater when individuals are ready to sacrifice their temporary advantage for the benefit of others in the group. In thriving communities, the members are anxious to contribute, often without reward in kind. Communities die when most members are primarily interested only in what they personally can get out of their participation. On the other hand, a community relationship is most effective when it is, to a large degree, mutual, with reciprocal bonds among its members, and with a common purpose that all can support.

Regretfully, however, communities act like composite individuals, in that there is still the inclination to fear, the instinct for brute survival, and the accompanying sense of competition and conflict with other communities. It is only the action of individuals with broad consciousness that can achieve a choice other than that old 'program'. Their concerted efforts must direct the action of the community to reflect their somewhat more developed consciousness. The community attitude must be made into that which results from the leaders' consciousness that is hopefully based on broader reflections in space and time.

In ancient times, people spoke of 'priests, prophets, and kings' as major roles in communities. There are many analogs, but in today's more democratic society, we think of servers, teachers, and leaders. In some way, every one of us is all three. We all serve, hopefully selflessly, the interests of others, at least sometimes; we clarify or explain (and so teach) when needed; and we also speak out in protest when needed, (and so lead) at times. Of course, we often serve as workers assisting in these functions. In all these roles, and many more, the practice of empathy, caring love, and kindness builds trust among those with whom we work. A mutual respect develops, which encourages the practice of truthfulness, and openness. The result can be bonds of affection and cooperation that are strong and deep.

Interlocking Communities

A person may participate in many distinct communities, simultaneously. However, there is a physical limit. When a stone is tossed into a still pond, the ripples are greatest at the center, and diminish with distance, even though some effect may reach the farthest corners. Similarly, a person has strong consciousness-interactions primarily in a limited sphere, with lesser interactions over greater spaces, because caring love usually involves the expenditure of large amounts of time and energy.

In many cases, this central peak of consciousness is in the core community called the family. Family members become very close to one another. This is especially true with spouses that are fully committed to each other. This conjugal love has a dimension of its own, arising from the sense of unity that years of sharing and mutual support can develop. It is this unity binding the couple, often accompanied by an awareness of their joint unity with a Divine Providence, that constitutes marriage. That unity is an on-going process, not miraculously created by the 'statement of intent' in the marriage ceremony. Rather, it is built, often with great effort, through the innumerable decisions and acts of love over the years.

In every community, be it extended-family, club, or tribe, there can be some mutual bonds of empathy, kindness, and love. The degree to which consciousness bonds exist determines the degree of true community. The world-view, then, is that of myriads of communities, each striving to grow in community spirit, with each person a member of multiple communities. The ideal is a sense of community that is strong for local groups and yet is global to a sufficient degree. Since the physical limitations and the inclinations to brute survival both foster local optimization, the struggle is to achieve a sufficient degree of non-local or global consciousness, while we foster the more intimate local consciousness.

One can consider these interlocking communities, that are truly based on bonds of consciousness, to be a prime expression of God's creation. We can admire God's handiwork in the entirety, - throughout nature, and finally in the many aspects of mutual support, empathy, wisdom, mercy, and creative use of power, that are found in the human community. All these communities participate in the evolution towards cooperative unity with the one God. All contribute to a gradual universal communion. Yet they operate creatively, in freedom, resisting pressures to uniformity. Hence each part grows to fulfillment in communion with the others. When we stand back and look at the wonder of this, we feel the need for participation in this dream of God's. Aware of

Figure 3: The Growth of Communities

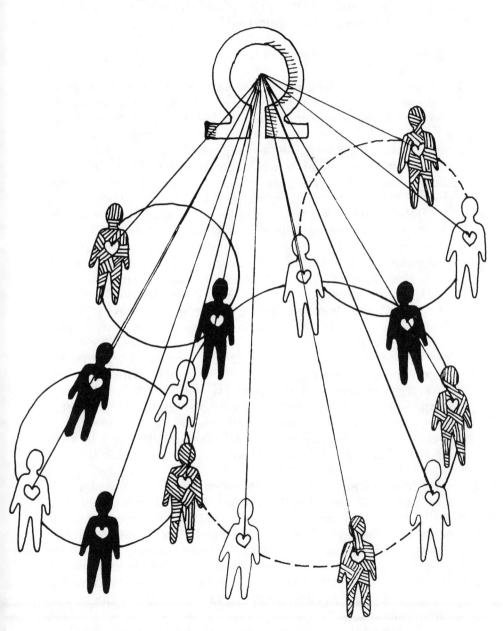

this, how can we slide carelessly out of a marriage? How can we mug another member of the human race? How can we undermine the self-confidence of the oppressed?

Church As Community

A major source of inspiration and support in this pilgrimage to true community can be a church. A church is a community of people that share the adoption of the hypothesis of the existence of God, and commit their way of life to harmony with that hypothesis. This hypothesis, we suggested, can be expressed as that direction-setting force which gently urges the evolution of consciousness to ever higher levels. In the church community there develops a common trust in this Divine Providence.

Every event, then, whether of joy or suffering, can be seen in this context of potentially moving towards a higher good. From every situation, there is still the possibility of exercising or promoting a higher level of consciousness. There is that trust that the highest level of consciousness, that of God, is ever present. Trust, in turn generates the hope that, no matter how deep the current suffering, there is available the strength to move forward. That inner strength enables one to pass through the current difficulties, and to continue on this evolutionary path, to exercise and grow our consciousness. A church community, moreover, helps to nurture the trust that the fulfillment of humankind, in the long term growth of consciousness, will in fact materialize. Despite retrogressions, despite failures, despite all current weaknesses and distractions, despite all calamities, this growth has evidently been proceeding. A church community helps to keep alive the hope that this growth will continue to proceed, by its trust in the Divine Providence.

Confidence in the Divine Providence is sometimes similarly applied to confidence in the evolution of the church community itself, at least as far as its own evolution of consciousness is concerned. There is the trust that despite the weaknesses, failures, mistakes, and errors of its members or its leaders, the ultimate progress of the community will continue, under the influence of Divine Providence. The church, in turn, then aspires to be the leaven that helps to raise the consciousness of the entire world-community.

The example of Jesus in promoting fraternity in community is worth noting. As John P. Egan writes: "In deep trouble with the

power structure of his day, Jesus shares a seder meal with his
closest friends. ... He takes off his clothes and washes feet, the feet
of his friends. His act radically breaks the illusory distinction
between slave and free, superior and inferior. Such distinction
separates human from human and puts chains on us all".[13]

The churches of the poor, especially, seem to retain this spirit
of fraternity. Boff writes:

> All are called to be 'people' and not just a subordinate class.
> Human beings achieve this in the measure to which, through
> the mediations of communities, they cease to be a mass,
> develop self-consciousness, lay out a historical plan for
> justice and participation for all (and not only for themselves),
> and teach practices that lead to the prompt realization of this
> utopia. ... The 'base ecclesial community' is generally made
> up of 15-20 families. They get together once or twice a week
> to hear the word of God, to share their problems in common,
> and to solve those problems through the inspiration of the
> Gospel. ... There is no noncharismatic member; ...all enjoy
> equal dignity; there is no room for privileges that destroy the
> unity of the whole. ... No one is to be called master, teacher,
> or spiritual director, because all are brothers and sisters (cf.
> Matthew 23:8-10). ... The principal characteristic of this way
> of being Church is community. Everyone is a true brother
> and sister; all share in common tasks ... through the direct
> participation of all the members of the group, the sharing of
> responsibilities, leadership, and decision-making, through
> the exercise of power as service. ... The basis of these
> communities is the word of God that is heard and reread
> within the context of their real problems; they are held
> together by their faith, their communitarian projects, their
> helping one another, and their celebrations.[14]

Regrettably, these teachings of fraternity and service are not
always followed, even in those communities that call themselves
church. Nevertheless, we see many examples of loving church-
related communities where the primary activities are service to
others and the simple joy of sharing an awareness of God's love.
There, the community supports the growth of consciousness in all
of its members. The sense of a way of life leading to salvation is
clarified.

Belonging to a church is often an experience that is difficult to express. It may be the result of profound inspiration by some charismatic leader. Then disciples stumble around trying to find the words to describe the persons or the principles which have so altered their lives. Nevertheless, the church helps each one to find some tentative answers to age-old questions, such as:

Who am I?

Possible answer:

I am a child of God, born with an inner thirst for goodness,- a spark that is the image and likeness of God.

What is my purpose?

Possible answer:

To grow in consciousness, to contribute to world consciousness, and so to contribute to the growth of God's spirit in the world.

How can I do this?

Possible answer:

By cleansing myself of negative attachments and negative emotions, and by practicing my fundamental option of empathy, caring love, and kindness.

With the support of a church community, we all seek to grow ourselves and also to be part of the larger community growth. We thus all seek to free the spirit of God within ourselves and through our participation, allow the building of that spirit in our communities. For Christians, Paul (Ephesians 4:15) put it this way:

If we live by the truth and in love, we shall grow in all ways into Christ, who is the head by whom the whole body is fitted and joined together, every joint adding its own strength, for each separate part to work according to its function. So the body grows until it has built itself up, in love.

3.7 WE SHALL BECOME

As the above discussion of evil, suffering, and forgiveness indicates, the further creation of ourselves and the kind of world we strive for is not without pain. The dream is nevertheless to become all that we are capable of, with full consciousness, maximizing the good in all the space and time we can perceive. That dream does not fulfill itself. The dream needs to be fulfilled by us, by our own 'blood, sweat, and tears'. In doing this, we seize the initiative, and enjoy the elation of self-fulfillment, as we contribute to a grander plan. The purpose and meaning of all this is stabilized by our grateful acknowledgment of God, as the benevolent force that gradually draws the universe towards greater complexity and consciousness.

In this process, we each have a creative role, and a birthing role, contributing directly to the continuing evolutionary growth of consciousness. Exercising the fabulous gift of free will, every one of us can choose a constructive course, despite the distractions and attractions of built-in 'programs'.

Not seeking suffering, we nevertheless can partake of the empathy and compassion which suffering generates. Trying not to acquiesce to violence of any kind, we also learn to forgive; and we strive to join in the building of consciousness with those who need our forgiveness. Remembering the great faith God has in us, and his abiding love for us, we learn to forgive ourselves, and to struggle on. We reach out to be with others, and to contribute to others in many kinds of relationships. These communities, too, help to build ourselves and others.

All this flourishes in the free exercise of empathy, caring love, and kindness. People naturally sense that this vibrant way of living brings fulfillment in accord with the Divine plan. They believe that in this way, the growth of that spark of God within all of us, is, somehow, part of the birth of 'how it is meant to be' on this earth.

REFERENCES

[1]Huston Smith, *Forgotten Truth*, Harper and Row, New York, 1977, p. 53.
[2]Matthew Fox, *Original Blessing*, Bear & Co., Santa Fe, New Mexico, 1983, pp. 221–222.

[3]Huston Smith, *The Religions of Man*, Harper and Row, New York, 1958, p. 27.

[4]Bukkyo Dende Kyokai, *The Teachings of Buddha*, Sangodo Printing Co., Ltd. Tokyo, seventeenth edition, 1972.

[5]W. Henry Keney, *A Path Through Teilhard's Phenomenon*, Pflaum Press, Dayton, Ohio, 1970.

[6]Ginny Desmond Billinger, *Pro-Life Feminism: Different Voices*, le Books, 1985.

[7]Jay Mc Daniel, "The God of the Oppressed and the God Who Is Empty", *Journal of Ecumenical Studies*, vol. 22 no. 4, Fall, 1985, p. 696.

[8]H. Kung, *Signposts For the Future*, Doubleday & Co., Garden City, N.Y., 1978, p. 15.

[9]Jay Mc Daniel, *loc. cit.*, p. 697.

[10]T.A.Harris, *I'm O.K. You're O.K.*, G.K.Hall, Boston, 1974.

[11]H. Kung, *Signposts For the Future*, Doubleday & Co., Inc, New York, 1978, p. 11.

[12]L.Rasmussen, "Patriotism Lived: Lessons From Bonhoeffer", *Christianity and Crisis*, June 24,1985, pp. 249–254.

[13]John P. Egan: "The 'Hood' is the Problem With Priesthood", *National Catholic Reporter*, April 19, 1985.

[14]Leonardo Boff, *Church: Charism & Power*, Crossroad, New York, 1985, pp. 117, 121, 125, 128, 129, 139, 140, 157, 158.

4

CHALLENGES AND
OPPORTUNITIES

As was mentioned in Chapter 1, every hypothesis needs to be continually tested, to see in what range of circumstances it continues to give good results. So too, if growth in consciousness is to be our fundamental option, it must give good results in life's practical and difficult problem areas. In this and the following chapter, we examine some important areas from this point of view.

Our emotions and our physical makeup often seem to control our lives, so let's first have a look at that aspect. We suggest that consciousness is fundamentally important to living fully with our emotions and physiology. Salt dissolves in water and affects the taste of every drop; so too, as one grows in empathy, caring-love, and kindness, these can affect all levels of consciousness, and help to steer emotions and passions accordingly.

We usually consider emotions an obstacle. However, every obstacle also turns out to be an opportunity for creative application of our highest levels of consciousness. Daily obstacles test and strengthen our consciousness. Controlling our emotions in ordinary, every day life is, therefore, pertinent to our growth and the growth of consciousness in the world.

4.1 PHYSIOLOGY AND DECISION

Some Common Mechanisms

Actions like caring, forgiveness, and community-cooperation require decisions based on a perception of what is around us.
Particularly in times of stress, these decisions are often affected by
our emotions, as well as by our intellect. To feel fully alive and
free, we need to feel that we are in command of ourselves, and not
slaves to the demands of unwanted emotions. We need to feel
capable of making the decisions we truly want, rather than those
which emotions press on us. Therefore, we had better observe and
try to understand a bit about how our physiological reactions
could aid or impede our exercise of consciousness.

We are all probably familiar with the 'fight or flight' phenomenon. Apparently, long ago, survival depended on it. A small
stimulus, indicating danger of some sort, can arouse strong
physiological reactions in a very short time, that enable us to
quickly fight or flee. Today, those massive reactions are still
largely present, but we usually neither fight nor flee. Our pulse
rate still goes up; our blood pressure increases; our blood vessels
constrict; and many other body-effects can be observed. But, we
try to retain our 'cool' and cope with the situation in a civilized
fashion. The lack of a 'normal' fight or flight outlet, however, can
result in a build-up of tension, stress, and general emotional
discomfort. Thus, while physiological reactions are exceedingly
valuable at times, they can also cause great distress and reduce our
capabilities. On the other hand, we each have the capability to
control this stress, and it's part of our creative task to do so.

A second well-studied phenomenon is that of positive feedback. We know that if we are talking into a microphone, for
example, and if the loudspeaker is too close to the microphone,
then we'll get a loud squeal. The amplified voice is fed back into
the microphone, is amplified again, and so forth. In a somewhat
similar way, it appears that recollections of the effects of earlier
stimuli can become stimuli themselves. Thus, an emotion can also
build up through the positive feedback of recollections, particularly if the emotion is one that causes fear, anger, anxiety, or
stimulated pleasure. Higher levels of stress may result from such
a build-up of stimuli. We generally know when that escalation is
occurring, and we have the ability, using a higher level of

consciousness, to see what's happening; then we can nip it in the bud by putting our attention elsewhere.

Another observation is that stress, while quickly generated, is not as quickly dissipated. In fact, the residual stress can last for hours or even days, and may require considerable physical exercise and/or relaxation to dissipate it. Moreover, repeated stimulations can result in higher levels of stress and longer retention of stress. Hence, what we refer to as habits may have associated physiological sequences, whose patterns are largely determined by prior events. We need to develop the ability to exercise full consciousness despite these handicaps.

We evidently also operate with a kind of parallel processing. We can drive our car and chew gum and think about where we are going, essentially simultaneously. On the other hand, we can, if we're not careful, forget where we're going, and simply drive, drive, and drive. The higher levels of consciousness can't be asleep for long, in such circumstances, or damage may result!

Our different levels of consciousness have a sort of semi-autonomy. Roughly, it seems like the auto-pilot of the airplane which enables the system to proceed without much intervention by the pilot. On the other hand, there is the ability of the pilot to oversee these operations and to affect these operations when necessary. So, too, we can allow ourselves to continue in certain habitual patterns of thought and actions. But, with sufficient effort, there is the ability for higher levels of consciousness to be aware of what the lower level cycles are all about, and to influence those patterns.

Coping

There apparently is no way to eliminate all disturbing physiological effects. Nor would we want to, for our emotions are basically good and necessary. In many cases, we are delighted by and celebrate their effects. Nevertheless, we know that they must often be bridled and carefully directed. Sometimes it seems as if our small craft were regularly beset by strong winds, waves, and tides. We know from experience that we can travel through them, and we can recover our course, continuously, if the direction is clear and our resolve to recover is firm and confident. Practice in the curtailment and redirection of stress is necessary, as in any other skill. Successful recoveries and growing confidence build courage to persevere against still greater storms. When each 'battle' is passed, one's sense of personhood grows stronger.

We need an interior, higher-level, program that can displace external pressures. Ouspensky observes:

> Although emotion is much quicker than thought, emotion is a temporary thing, but thought can be made continuous; so whenever the emotion jumps out, it hits against this continuous thought and cannot go on and manifest itself. So you can struggle with the expression of negative emotions...only by creating continuous right thinking.[1]

Honest self esteem is the foundation of the ability to cope. The lack of self esteem, and the feeling of inadequacy, may be due to repeated negative experiences or recollections. Our minds record words, pictures, and emotions. If we re-think negative experiences, the recordings reinforce a negative view of the world. We thus also build a negative and false view of ourselves. The antidote is to deliberately see the best in ourselves. Knowing we're O.K., really valuable persons, and beloved by God, prevents panic and instills quiet confidence.

We also need to work steadily to see ourselves not in a desperate battle for survival, and not in a struggle for dominance over others, but rather in a common constructive cause. Again, it would seem, the constant pursuit of full consciousness of other persons, in a spirit of empathy, caring love, and kindness, is an effective policy. It not only provides the long term direction, but also offers a ready displacement of, or antidote to, many emotions.

Negative emotions like rage, jealousy, and fear usually involve some kind of permission from ourselves. It is helpful to remember that the control and/or the extension of such emotions are within us and not in other people, - they are internal, not external. These negative emotions can be crowded out as we seek a broader perspective and deliberately substitute a more positive train of thought. One can thus redirect the energies of an emotion from a more primitive aim to one that is ethically or culturally at a higher level. The inner resources for this evidently are great when one reaches deeply for them.

Some measures to directly relax our bodies also may help. One's higher levels of consciousness can, in fact, control one's body to a surprising extent. Simply being aware of tension in a specific part of the body, and deliberately relaxing that muscle can have immediate results. An often recommended practice is to slowly scan the body mentally, from head to toe, relaxing each portion in turn. The muscles throughout the body will respond to this. Another good illustration is the 'waterfall cleansing' exercise. Imagine yourself approaching a cool, clean, sparkling waterfall on a warm day. Step into the waterfall, and imagine that you feel the cooling and cleansing effects all over your body. Then imagine the cool, cleansing water pouring all through the interior of your body, - through every passage, every item, every molecule. Celebrate the cleansing action. Know that you are being 'cleansed' of all stress, all dirt, all needless guilt. Again, the effects on the entire body can be remarkable, and need to be experienced to be believed.

Though we apparently have 'parallel processing' of different levels of our consciousness (as described above), our highest level seems to be purely sequential, - that is, we can handle only one thought train at a time at the highest level. If we are distracted, then the highest level is completely devoted, at least momentarily, to that distraction. That highest level is our most precious re- source, and therefore, one would be inclined to invest its use wisely rather than frivolously.

Also important, therefore, is the control of what enters our minds, which may needlessly upset our emotional balance. The phrase: "garbage in/garbage out" sums it up. If we allow our minds to be filled with demanding and persistent distractions, the control of stress is more difficult, and our output will be condi- tioned by the distracting garbage. Rather than consume our time and energies in yielding to distractions or in combatting them, it is often wiser to not grant them initial entry to our minds. Rather than passively submitting ourselves to the demands of external garbage, we need to apply ourselves to the active construction of a positive viewpoint. For example, we can reach out, beyond our current distractions, for a view of a broader horizon, and direct our energies there. Or, we can turn our minds away from the garbage to appreciate the grandeur of creation in that very setting; we can move our minds to consider the beauty of all that has been created, and be thankful for it.

Finally, perhaps the most important ingredient in our coping with stress can be a sense of trust in God's care. This can be effective in reducing anxiety and the stress it causes. Trust involves the awareness that we are not alone, that God intends our growth and passage through current difficulties. We have freely 'joined God's team'; and we believe that this partnership will result in our eventual fulfillment. Then, opening ourselves to God's inspiration, and expecting God's loving care, we can work more effectively as stress drains from our bodies.

In trusting God, we open ourselves to guidance by an inner divine spirit. It's like letting the horse help us to find the way home. We perceive being part of a broader context, and a larger process under divine providence. Our bodies take a different stance. The tightness of fear unbends. A new body-felt sense of life and hope can result.

Thus, in summary, it's necessary that each of us develops some skill in coping with physiological pressures. Fortunately, as humans, we do have an inherent higher level capability to consciously decide things; and this can be used to offset these physiological effects before they become dominant. Basic to a good decision is the seeking of the broader view, in space or time. Often this involves the considered application of empathy, caring love and kindness to all parties. Finally, then, we can get strength from a trust in God's caring love and his desire for our success. Coping with physiological effects thus becomes part of our growth and part of the growth of world consciousness.

4.2 JEWELS OR DEHUMANIZERS?

There are, obviously, many things in life which have great potential for good or evil, depending on how they are used. Three, however, have frequently been cited as playing major roles, for good or evil, for personal fulfillment or personal destruc- tion, - namely: money, sex, and authority. Most of us think of these with relish, and feel that more is better. On the other hand, many religious orders have singled out three corresponding vows to avoid evil, - namely, vows of poverty, chastity, and obedience. Money, sex, and authority can affect our lives so directly and frequently that they deserve careful attention. Let's examine them in the light of the mission of growing consciousness.

4.3 MONEY

The Bible story (Matthew 19:23) relates how difficult it is for a rich man to enter into heaven. Surely, there's a message here. Is it that no one should have possessions? Is the possession of 'riches' itself immoral? Or does their possession somehow block the pursuit of goodness?

Again, let's try to use the ideal of maximizing consciousness as a reference. Given that we have a certain amount of riches, we may use that wealth with a narrow or a broad viewpoint. We may consider only ourselves, and maximize the benefit that riches can give to us. Or, we may be conscious of larger and larger spheres, in space and time, and appropriately use our wealth to maximize the benefit over these larger spheres, including others and future consequences. The existence of wealth gives one the opportunity to use it for broad purposes, and that use would seem to affect the degree to which we achieve our ideal of maximizing consciousness.

A problem with money, however, is that it can become addictive, in that its possession promotes a focus on it. This tends to narrow our focus so that we may ignore everything but the preservation or accumulation of wealth. In that narrow focus, it is difficult to use the wealth to maximize benefit in the larger spheres. There is a tendency to put down, disparage, and demean those who do not have equal wealth. The accumulation of wealth can even become the objective, at the expense of starvation, suffering, and loss of personal dignity of many others. One has to admit that this is a strong inclination, which makes the Biblical observation understandable.

Despite this apparent difficulty, however, other facts remain. Crime is far from being absent among the really poor. If anything, real poverty often leads to degradation, desperation, and violence. Furthermore, the stability of wealth at least gives the opportunity for putting into action the empathy, love, and hence kindness, that characterize a broad consciousness. Wealth, therefore, has the potential for good. The challenge is the same challenge faced in the long process of growing consciousness: to resist the tendency to local optimization and local addiction.

The pursuit of profit as a means to the broader fulfillment of all persons must replace the idolatry of profit as the only end goal. The virtue of being 'poor in spirit', can then be expressed constructively. Avoiding a narrow fixation on wealth itself, being 'poor in spirit' can be the treatment of wealth as a platform from which one can nurture others and enable empathetic consciousness.

4.4 SEX AND MARRIAGE

Of all life's properties, sex is perhaps both the most extolled and maligned. In the media, it's the best and the worst. We're drawn to it and fearful of it. Where is the balance? Above all, we have to recognize that we are God's creation. Hence, all of our being and all of our capabilities have an inherent goodness and beauty, and a great potential for creating further good. So we can accept our sexuality thankfully, respect it, and cherish it as God's beautiful gift. We can be at peace, on friendly terms (and not at war) with ourselves and all of our God-given sexual capabilities. We need then to discern how to best use the gifts we have been given, so as to maximize the good and to harmonize our use with God's plan for our true fulfillment.

The media would often have us believe that love and sex are synonymous. Obviously there's a big difference, and that difference is crucial. True caring love is often confused with 'falling in love' that may be only physically motivated. This latter, obviously, has a very constructive role in life, but by itself it is transitory in comparison with caring love, and is no substitute for the latter. It seems to us that caring love builds personhood and produces a permanent growth in the person. Sexually motivated, purely romantic love, if it is without a caring love, does not. Nevertheless, sexually motivated and caring love complement each other. They facilitate each other, and the combination brings a unique unity and enrichment.

The Dark and the Bright Sides of Sex

Sex has both a bright and a dark side; let's first look at the dark side. As with wealth, we find that there can be an unfortunate tendency to narrow one's focus, and so sex can similarly become a narrow addiction. (Too narrow a focus, on even a good thing, it seems, may be harmful.) It may cause us to lose sight of a larger good, which may be more important. In particular, too narrow a focus on sex can distract one from the reality of the larger personality; and one can very easily lose sight of the other person's internal beauty and potential as a child of God. On the other hand, that broader awareness can be maintained. Humankind, in good health, can perform remarkably well in breaking out of a limited view; in the bright sunlight of total reality, the narrow focus is eliminated by placing sex in the larger picture of a truly loving relationship. At least a potential advantage of a good marriage is that the years of mutual experience can build a deeper awareness of this inner worth of the partner; the beauty of the sexual relationship then can be in harmony with the larger awareness of total worth.

An obsession with food leads to obesity. An over indulgence in sex, while also considered gross, leads to more subtle distortions. When not treated properly, sex can become an intrusion into any aspect of our lives and a distraction from higher levels of consciousness. The subconscious that is overly stimulated in sexual matters intrudes to consume a larger fraction of one's attention. This can effectively distract from a focus at higher levels of consciousness, obstruct the practice of empathy, and hence inhibit growth of consciousness. It's essential, therefore, that the 'golden mean of all things in moderation' be followed in this regard, and that we develop the skill of redirecting our energies elsewhere, when appropriate.

Having recognized all that, however, one should also emphasize the very positive roles sex plays, and that it can be consciousness-raising and truly beautiful. Our sexuality, including its sensuality and passion, is a good gift and a real blessing from God. It was lovingly imparted to all of nature, even before the arrival of the human species, "and it was good" (Genesis 1:31). Humankind have been given additional gifts, making them capable of higher consciousness. That consciousness enables us to modulate those former gifts, and to *steer* that energy so that with mind, body, and spirit, we try to maximize empathy, caring love, and kindness in the use of our sexuality.

The Conscious Marriage

Like so many other things in life, sex needs to be lifted to a higher context, in order to obtain its full beauty. Within a framework of real love and a strong commitment to each other, sex can be a joyful expression of solidarity, involving total trust, genuine dedication, humble giving, and a great respect and appreciation for each other. Though each person retains a precious individuality, and each strives to preserve and enhance the self worth and distinct dignity of the other, the sense of common purpose can be great. As a strong state of mutual support and sharing is built, sex can be a facilitator of reconciliation, a joyful expression of unity, and a strengthening of it. A strong commitment to the well-being of the other can encompass minds and hearts; and the unity of the bodies is then a very natural and wholesome complement, rather than something separate.

Teilhard de Chardin refers, almost poetically, to the great potential of this 'spiritualized love', in the following:

> Love, as well as thought, is always in full growth...The excess of its expanding energy over the daily diminishing needs of human propagation is daily becoming more evident. This means that love is tending, in its fully hominized form, to fulfill a much larger function than the mere call to reproduction. Between Man and Woman a specific and reciprocal power of sensitization and spiritual fertilization seems in truth to be still slumbering, demanding to be released in an irresistible upsurge towards everything which is truth and beauty.[2]

Sex can also be an expression of a unity with all of creation and its divine author. Praising the goodness and beauty of each other can be accompanied by thanking God for his goodness and the beauty of all he has created. The caring couple thus can make sex a sign of their commitment to be in harmony with each other at all levels of their being, and so also in harmony with their understanding of the divine plan. Greeley and Durkin put it even more strongly:

> We make love to our lover and at the same time we make love to God because...the other's being participates and inheres in God's Being....All love affairs in the Catholic tradition of sacramentality are *menage a trois*.[3]

Sacramental it is, as we see the work of God in each other and the sacredness of each other. The intimacy and deep affection is thus seen as a reflection of God's own intimate love and affection for us.

Thus, more adequate marriages are not limited to reciprocal sexual satisfaction for both parties; the relationship involves deep personal friendship, mutual support, and shared spiritual growth of the spouses. It also involves strong ties of love with other members of the family; and it may further extend its love and protection to persons outside the family, - for example to the

Figure 4: Total Love Can Involve the Total Person —
Physical, Emotional, Mental and Spiritual

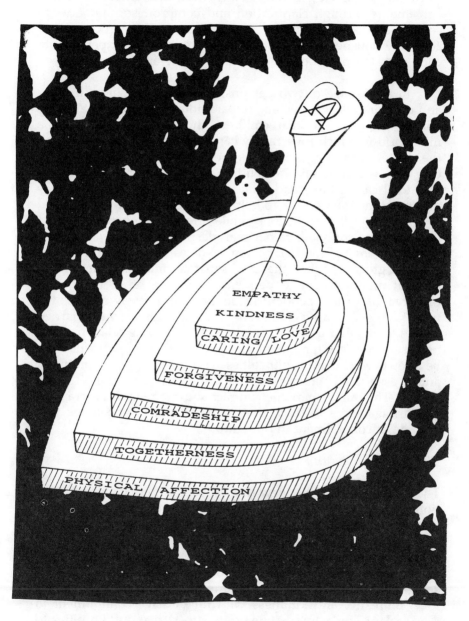

forlorn or the handicapped. Gaffney writes, "Spouses have to learn the social arts of partnership, how to cultivate practical agreements through clarification and compromise, and how to cope with disagreement by mutually acceptable procedures."[4] This consciousness of the other then provides the experience to cope with the needs of the extended family and people in need anywhere.

In a marriage of two persons, the well-being of each other and of their children, become of paramount importance. As they join to produce and rear children, they also join to create a miniworld in which their family can find true fulfillment. Within the shelter of marriage, each has the opportunity to be his or her true self, which involves extending oneself towards total empathy, total caring love, and total kindness. More than that, they may combine their efforts to help spread fulfillment in the world at large. But all this is done while strengthening the sense of individual personhood, rather than destroying it.

Truly loving another person involves the will to foster the spiritual growth of the other as a separate, independent person, without an inordinate dependency. On the other hand, this preservation of independent personhood in no way reduces the need for a very strong commitment to each other. Every married couple learns that a deep commitment to a loving relationship is necessary to allow time for stepwise growth. The path will often be strewn with painful difficulties, and only a real commitment and its associated perseverance will bring long term results to both parties. The public marriage contract and the religious sacrament of marriage serve to teach that message and to encourage that attitude of commitment in our culture.

The Virtue of Chastity

There is, of course, the view that celibacy fosters greater dedication to the will of God. This is often true; but we think it is not necessarily true in the broader perspective of total consciousness development. We know that service to the plan of God is possible in both the celibate and the married states; we have great examples in both categories. Moreover, the love, dedication, and sacrifice for spouse and family are unmatched training grounds for love, empathy, and kindness, and for decisive commitment to God's plan. The married state offers superlative opportunities to literally be Christ in the exercise of the way that he taught.

Moreover, if a married person, male or female, can dedicate time and effort to serving God as lay minister, deacon, priest, or other servant, we do think God would find that service pleasing. On the other hand, marriage is not for everyone. It would make more sense, we think, to have optional celibacy in more forms of religious vocations.

Somewhat stronger on this point is the Jewish view that:

> Both the sympathetic understanding of man's needs, and the view that the material world was of divine origin, combined to make it a religious obligation to enjoy life and the bounties of God's creation. Indeed, it has been said that "He who sees a legitimate pleasure and does not avail himself of it is an ingrate against God who made it possible."[5]

To sum up, it seems that every pleasure in life finally gives lasting joy and personal satisfaction only to the extent that it is in harmony with and supportive of our higher consciousness. With that illumination, things are different. It's like seeing the full beauty of things in the bright sunlight; and one acts accordingly. It is no surprise, therefore, that the delightful self-expression, play, and joy that are derivable in intimate sexual encounters are similarly enriched and given new meaning in empathetic and caring love of married couples. Thus, we suggest that *whether sex is a purely mechanical, and perhaps demeaning intrusion, or a supporting and wholesome reinforcement, depends in large part on the degree of active empathy, caring-love, kindness, (E.L.K.) and freedom that is retained at higher levels.* In some circumstances, where sexual desire is an unwanted distraction, strong E.L.K. are an effective substitute for these distractions. In other circumstances, the emphasis on E.L.K. steers the sexual emotions so that they reinforce constructive inter-personal relations. The lower, more mechanical pleasure, in other words, is best subordinate to and at times supportive of the higher, more conscious pleasure.

The virtue of chastity, in this light, is not limited to the narrow abstinence from all aspects of sex. Rather, it can be the careful use or non-use of sex, being very conscious of the precious personhood and inherent dignity of the other. The virtuous use of sex can be an effective means for the further development of joint consciousness. In a range of complex sexual interactions, the dedicated couple naturally can develop a shared consciousness of each other and beyond. In particular, that shared consciousness can include a joint sense of unity with one's creator through the amazing beauty of that creation.

The Optimum Family ?

Family size is another good example where local optimization is not sufficient and a broader perspective is increasingly needed. Most agree that the primary role of sex is reproduction, with the joys of love and sacrifice in the raising of children that it entails. There is no joy comparable to that of a loving family. This is well understood; and we need to take that fact fully into account, but in the light of a broad consciousness.

One has to also address the issue of how large a family, and family planning. Some would hold that things like empathy, caring love, and kindness are naturally fostered in the family, and therefore, the larger the family the better. Unfortunately, things are not that simple. Few would say that there is a mandatory rush to populate heaven, right now, regardless of the suffering caused. For example, few would argue that it is compassionate to bring another million starving babies into the devastation of Ethiopia today. Also, our prisons are full of people who never had sufficient love from their parents, in families too large to be supported economically or lovingly. In money, time, and energy, there's just so much to go around; and beyond some family size, children may not get the care and the training they need. With sufficient neglect, the result often is a general decrease of consciousness in the family, and the well being of those affected by the family.

If, as we've suggested, our objective should be to maximize the empathy, caring love, and kindness, in all the space and time that we have anything to do with, then we should ask ourselves what size family will do that. This is a classic example of where broad consciousness may require parents to constrain one good in order to promote a broader or higher good. This limitation may seem to be a lessening of good, if one is content with local optimization, at that time and in that space. In a broader context, however, it may be seen as very positive. Each couple therefore is asked to consider the total good that is sought and the total effects.

For each couple there is an analysis and a decision needed on the issue of family size. How will the number of children in the average family affect the lives of the couples, the families, and the larger community, both now and during the coming generations? It is not a trivial decision that can be neglected. Even if a precise answer to this question is impossible, a best judgement is required. This stretches our ability to think in broader space and time. It requires a sense of community; some nations even have guidelines on it, on the assumption that they are for the health of the nation. Many are persuaded that there is a moral relevance of public interest to private reproductive choices. It's not sufficient to allow this to be a momentary decision; it takes reflective thought and time to percolate. It's the kind of issue that only humankind has the capability to address. It's both a challenge and a privilege. Thus, we are convinced that thoughtful, careful, family planning is a very serious moral responsibility of every couple; the couple can exercise a high degree of broad consciousness and contribute meaningfully to the optimization of the total creation process.

Counter-Cultural Sex

Premarital sex, homosexuality, and abortion are topics which challenge us to take a new look and to honestly reassess the issues in the best light we can provide. Like many other important issues, these need the broadest consciousness we can muster and, in turn, help to stretch us to still broader consciousness.

For a very long time, pre-marital sex has been considered counter-cultural. Now, there is a trend to accept this as more 'normal' behavior. Is this only a question of perspective and environment? What does it have to do with the fundamental issues of building the loving community? While it is not possible to generalize for all situations, it appears to be clear that many cases have much in common. If we look dispassionately at this, don't we frequently find that in pre-marital sex, people are mistreating other people; that they are treating one another simply as sex objects; and that they are ignoring possible consequences to present or potentially future individuals? When that is true, the damage would seem to be enormous; but there's more. Promiscuous sexual relations have proven to have horrifying physical and mental consequences. Debilitating and fatal diseases, and severe psychological damage defy the best efforts of our medical professions. Syphilis, gonorrhea, and now AIDS acquire epidemic proportions where promiscuity becomes widespread. More than this, however, is the problem of the possibility of a child by any of these thoughtless actions, without the family community to enable it to be a loved child. This brings up the whole community concept of protection of the weaker members of the community; pre-marital sex potentially violates this concept. It frequently is simply a case of not treating present people as whole persons, and also exposing a possible future member of the community to serious deprivation of its right to a loving family. Empathy in space and time is lacking.

We are quick to add, however, that this is not necessarily always the case. Two persons can have a full and loving commitment to one another without the formal marriage contract. It certainly is conceivable that such a union, before marriage, between two mutually committed persons, can have more genuine empathy, caring love, and kindness than exists today in many marriages. It is, however, in our opinion, very difficult and rare to achieve a necessary level of sincerity and commitment in a short time, and without the sobering thoughtfulness and preparation that should accompany the public marriage commitment.

A second practice, which was heretofore considered to be counter-cultural, is that of homosexuality. This appears to be a more complex issue. It is generally assumed that this practice frequently is characterized by promiscuity and the emphasis on impersonal, recreational sex, at the purely physical level. Then all the above criticism applies; and that type of homosexuality is clearly a grave menace to the public health as well as the national culture. While this characterization may usually be very true, there is a growing belief that, in some cases, a long-term loving relationship may exist between two dedicated people of the same sex. Our culture, in most American cities, still discourages such relationships. We suggest that one must re-examine in charity the possibility of wholesome values, to the benefit of the individuals and the community, in some homosexual relationships.

The heterosexual marriage, can also be an extremely poor example of a community, with one party severely putting the other down and depriving the other of growth in full personhood. The battered spouse is too common to need elaboration, and the psychologically deprived spouse is vastly more common. Moreover, it would seem that God's love can be displayed in a community of two or more persons regardless of sex, each acting in loving and positive ways. Evidently both heterosexual and homosexual couples can be truly loving of each other or can treat the other as less than a person, and use the other primarily for selfish sexual gratification.

The fact is that God made us so that people need other people. The baby needs the touch of his mother's hand. Each person's psychological growth can benefit from close relationships with other persons. These needs normally are filled by the favored heterosexual marriage. But there are other cases. For a woman who has been beaten and otherwise mistreated by a father, there may be no possibility of a meaningful and loving relationship with a man. It may be a necessary thing for her to feel the comfort in the touch of another woman's hand, in order for her to really feel a part of humanity. Let us suppose that in a truly lasting and loving relationship, these two do go beyond accepted conduct and satisfy their sexual needs with each other. Are we to condemn them? Are there any harmful consequences to them or to the community at large from this private show of affection? It would seem that, as Rev. Charles Curran holds, acts should be judged not merely by their physical nature, but also in the context of the couple's relationship to one another, and the quality of the care they give.[6]

We don't pretend to have any simple answers to these complex problems. Many churches have taken a firm position that homosexuality is a disorder. In general that appears to be true. It is abundantly clear that promiscuous homosexual activities can be extremely dangerous. They can often have devastating psychological and physical effects on the individual, and can thwart the fundamental moves to higher consciousness. However, we do believe that the issues in particular cases are sometimes so unclear that we must leave open the charitable position that God understands and blesses some of these genuinely loving relationships.

A third cultural and moral issue, today, is that of abortion. Here, again, the heterosexual act too often can become an example of local optimization, at the expense of others. We often look at sex as only an interaction between two persons; yet, if there is any possibility of conception, is it not, to some degree, also an invitation to a third person? All too often, abortion, following sex, is simply likened to regurgitation following eating. Repugnant as that may be, it often neglects the empathy for the third party.

In our society, there are different opinions as whether one should consider the fetus to be a human being, or when it should be so considered. We are able to be empathetic to that being, if we believe it to be a growing baby. The person considering an abortion has the awesome responsibility to be conscious of what really exists. Surely that humanity is evident at some point in the pregnancy. If humanity at the time of conception is rejected, then

at what time does humanity begin? Can anyone rationally deny
the rights of that third human after it has developed to the point
of having a nervous system and sensory feelings? This humanity
is certainly evident when one sees the mutilated bodies of some
aborted fetuses which are so obviously babies in need of suste-
nance. If we are uncertain, what chances should one take with the
life of another?

If humankind's finest achievements and ultimate destiny
have to do with higher consciousness, doesn't this consideration
of a possible new baby demand the most empathy, love, and
kindness, of which we are capable? Should our empathy be
conditioned by the helplessness of that being, or by its degree of
perfection in our eyes? Doesn't it seem that attempts to simply
"retain control over one's body" in reality may be taking violent
control over another's body, and ignoring our very nature as
empathetic beings? That hardly seems imaginable when the
mother truly realizes she has a living baby. In every such case, it
seems to us, there must be a maximum effort to honestly discern
whether a human baby exists, a deep awareness of our need to be
fully human ourselves, and therefore an awakened empathy for
all those that are truly involved, in space and time.

We close this discussion of sex, the virtuous use of our
sexuality, the sacramental nature of that use, and the issues of
counter-cultural sex, with an observation by Greeley and Durkin:

> ...the only way to prevent abuse of the sexual dynamisms is
> to use those dynamisms as well as possible, as brilliantly, as
> imaginatively, as creatively, as passionately as one can.[7]

That best way, we suggest, is with maximum consciousness and
full awareness of the sacramental nature of it all.

4.5 AUTHORITY

The common view of authority is the right to command. It is a
power over others. Power is ego-building; and the inordinate
desire to obtain or retain power can be corrupting (as the history
of politicians amply proves). Nevertheless, the objective of authority is often a valuable good, - namely, the effective coordina-
tion of persons towards a worthwhile goal. The issue is how to

achieve these good ends without the pitfalls of an addiction to power or a misuse of power, while keeping in mind the growth of each person involved. The answer again, we feel, is in the exercise of consciousness, that is, caring concern, over space involving all participants, and over time involving future consequences. Proper authority, that yields good results for all, requires a combination of communion within community and the preservation of individuality and freedom.

Most persons need sufficient autonomy to build a sense of personal freedom, dignity, and growth, and to avoid a sense of restrictive domination. Hence, all authority structures need to be sensitive to the deep-seated yearnings for freedom of decision and participation in determining one's destiny. (This can be learned most clearly when trying to impose well-intended authority on teen-agers, who are less inhibited in expressing their needs for a degree of freedom and participation in decisions affecting them.) Those structures which are not sufficiently sensitive to this universal need are in fact an obstacle to fulfillment of that fundamental human need.

Hierarchy and Participative Management

The traditional authority structure is hierarchical. Often, one finds some simple notions of entitlement to a position of authority, and strict obedience of others to that position. That system can be effective, especially when one can nurture and placate a supportive constituency. It can be argued that blind obedience is a noble sacrifice to a higher good sought by all under the leadership of the hierarchy. This seems, in fact, to be real in some important cases. It can generate great loyalties, but it usually does not employ the full personhood of all the participants. It can be as Boff points out, "...the underlying conflict is one of the power of some over others, a power that will not abdicate its privileges and rights, at odds with the inviolable rights of human persons (participation, symbolic production, free expression, etc.)."[8] At its worst, it can be a subjugating and dehumanizing system.

People join large organizations, where their individuality may be submerged, inhibiting their growth. As organizations become larger, different distributions of authority have been tried. The trick is to still foster initiative, creativity, and personal fulfillment, and also to encourage cooperation and preserve an overall unity of purpose. In trying to achieve this, many organizations go through a growth process, on the way to maturity.

IBM, for example, was noted in its early years for its emphasis on conformity; proper hats, dark suits, and company songs were signs of this. This conformity served to develop a good sense of unity, in concert with an emphasis on a common set of ethics, and a highly centralized corporate authority. However, even with dedicated corporate officers and staff, it is physically impossible for them to be perceptive and sensitive to all the changing technologies and market opportunities in a large, growing, world-wide corporation. Bureaucracy inevitably results in stifled initiative, slow reaction times, and lost opportunities. More importantly, the sense of participation, and accompanying personal commitment and fulfillment, are diminished as the hierarchical structure grows.

A distribution of authority becomes necessary. As IBM grew, decentralization of profit responsibility was achieved, with nearly autonomous divisions, profit-centers, and independent business-units. Conformity was reduced, and diversity grew; but an overall unity was preserved with a more loose corporate structure and a continuing emphasis on ethics. Despite its size, the company has succeeded in promoting local initiative, and being flexible in responding to changing market conditions. A major reorganization, every two or three years, to meet changing needs, is quite common. Even with the very rapid changes, dislocations, and apparent turmoil, the company has managed to preserve a manifest respect for the individual. That results in an unusually high esprit de corps, which in turn fosters productivity, quality workmanship, and initiative.

Experience in many major organizations, in fact, shows that attempts to lead educated or well informed persons are effective only if done mainly by persuasion, and by consulting those who are going to have to implement the decision.[9] Authority, in this mode, is less hierarchical, less determinative, and more service-oriented. The logical extension, in many cases, is the fact that authority is *delegated upward*. As C. Bernard noted quite a long time ago: "As director of an organization, you have no power that is not granted to you by your subordinates. Eliciting their continuous (and, if possible, cheerful) cooperation is your main job as director; without it, you cannot get accomplished the most routine tasks."[10]

Modern industrial management techniques put great emphasis on the spirit of participation among all members of a task group. The objective is to make full use of the insights and creativity of the whole team, and to give each member a sense of responsibility for the success of the task. In this structure, blind obedience is a dereliction of duty. Rather, each member of the team has an obligation to use his or her full talents in the suggestion of direction and tactics, as well as in the execution of the task. Management, in these cases, must be shared, at least up to a point. The manager becomes more of a 'player-coach' or facilitator, and the players add a 'consulting' role to the execution of their duties. The entire team must be conscious of the team objective and the support that each provides to the total effort. So called 'quality-circles' are held periodically to encourage group discussion of problems and opportunities of improving task performance.[11] The emphasis is on treatment of all as responsible individuals, with increased opportunities for all to contribute. Enlightened management recognizes that such understanding of the needs of all workers, and appropriately considerate policies, are good for business.

On the other hand, experience also shows that there's a key place for real leadership. The inspired manager can lead his group, somewhat ahead of their consensus, once he discerns that a spirited leadership can convince them. Optimization, not for the moment, but for some longer view, is the leader's responsibility. Combining the advantages of leadership with the concern for the total well being and personal growth of all the participants is the challenge. Moreover, with rare exceptions, once all conflicting views are freely heard and amply considered, it's necessary that the spirit of teamwork take over in following the decision made by the manager. The sense of communion must remain even in that circumstance.

All of these examples have a common thread. The key success factors in industry depend on the use of our highest levels of consciousness. That involves an awareness of the needs of all participants, fostering free cooperation among peers, facilitating rather than demanding results, and the seeking of paths that maximize the good for all in space and time.

Authority and Church

Churches, too, naturally evolve in authority structures, but lacking the pressures of the marketplace, they evolve much more slowly. This can be an impediment to the personal fulfillment of church members.[12] In the earlier centuries, apostolic authority clearly rested in the entire college of bishops, in union with the successor to Peter. The teachings of the gospel emphasized fraternity rather than hierarchical orders: "You are one in Christ" (Galatians 3:26-29); "You are all brothers" (Matthew 23:8); "There must be no distinction between you" (James 2:2-4). However, as the centuries passed, more and more of the local authority was passed to the bishop of Rome, and a steady centralization of authority took place. The church conformed first to the Roman and then to the feudal systems of government. A serious distortion took hold.

Somehow the image of a loving, compassionate God that fosters personal growth took second place to an older image of a divine center of power and authority. The gentle teaching and inspiring modes used by Jesus were augmented by the exercise of power and authority. (A.N. Whitehead makes the point, with exaggeration, "The church gave unto God the attributes which belonged exclusively to Caesar."[13]) Orthodoxy and conformity in all shades of doctrine and liturgy often took precedence over compassion and free will. Authority by confrontation and coercion, frequently resulting in psychological and even physical violence, seemed to replace the mode of cooperation and comradeship in a common search for understanding. This, it was hoped, served to give a sense of unity to world-wide parishes. It also, however, did not promote the fundamental concept of a loving God who invites our free participation in the creative process. It caused many disasters, as in the East-West breach and in the famous Chinese Rites controversy in the 17th century.

Laws assumed an important place in the church operations. Some people reacted allergically against these laws, particularly when they felt the laws were being enforced more because of authoritarian attitudes than for convincing reasons. Other people looked for security in laws, and therefore were willing to adopt the legal culture. Still others strove for reform. For example, Saint Alphonsus (1696-1787), patron of moral theologians, firmly reminded his intolerant opponents, who seemed to know nothing other than law: "Imposing on others uncertain obligations is not a sign of holiness, but of arrogance and stubbornness." He warned those "zealots of rigidity" not "to chain and not to ensnare" the conscience of the faithful.[14]

The Eastern church also resisted the trend to centralized

authority, and still holds that authority of knowledge, or doctrine, rises from the consciousness of all the people. God's truth is said to be disclosed through the 'conscience of the church', meaning the thoughtful consensus of all Christians. It follows that initiatives from the bishops must stand the test of critical perception by the whole church. In practice, the crystallization of beliefs is often aided by the bishops who, as representatives of the people, attempt to focus the thought of the latter.

People of many faiths would now hold that even this process must be iterative. Granted that the inspiration of such a consensus may be the result of action by the Spirit of God acting through all the people; nevertheless, that Spirit must work through the limitations of humans, so that what is perceived is never pure. At a later time, persons with increased consciousness, or simply a different perspective, may be better able to respond to that inspiration.

Over the centuries, and especially since Vatican II, there have been many voices raised in the Catholic community to positively shift the emphasis from an excessive top-down authoritarianism and presumed finality, to a more creative evolution of understanding and pursuit of the fulfillment of man, as God intended. Fr. Gutierrez, for example, writes:

> Rather, the goal is ... above all to modify the emphasis, often obsessive, upon the attainment of an orthodoxy which is often nothing more than fidelity to an obsolete tradition or a debatable interpretation. In a more positive vein, the intention is to recognize the work and importance of concrete behavior, of deeds, of action, of praise in the Christian life.[15]

This is a shift in emphasis from centrally imposed uniformity to the concrete practice of virtues like empathy, caring love, and kindness. Creative initiatives, by individuals and groups, are used to meet pressing local needs.

The place for new views, and dissent from time-honored positions, still is the subject of much controversy. Nevertheless, awareness of the human potential, and of the responsibility to form critical judgements, has spread greatly. This results in encouragement of broad participation in the search for solutions to real life problems.

In some of the newer religious movements, too, a distribu-

tion of authority has proven to be stimulating and healthy.
Dinges, for example, states:

> The dramatic spread of Pentecostalism in third world coun-
> tries can be attributed to many factors, not the least of which
> is the fact that Pentecostalism creates organizations marked
> by social and religious equality and devoid of professiona-
> lized elites who monopolize core ritual symbols. Opportuni-
> ties for ministerial empowerment, and access and control
> over religious symbols are available to all at all ecclesial
> levels.[16]

Thus, in many religious areas there is a ferment towards flexible
and even egalitarian modes of operation. These are based on
greater respect for each individual and a greater empathy for the
needs of all.

The Evolution of Authority Modes

One can see that authority structures in all parts of society evolve
towards a greater degree of participation. In moving in that
direction, however, they must also try to balance a number of
opposing tendencies. John Langan says:

> Respect for the individual and the fostering of individual
> growth takes precedence, while leaving behind the notion of
> 'rugged individualism' that ignores the larger society.

> Assertiveness replaces cringing obedience, without falling
> into the trap of strident self knowledge.

> A communitarian ethos is accepted, but without that collec-
> tivism which loses sight of individual rights.

> Universality of common hopes and rights is accepted,
> without demanding uniformity of approaches.

> Pluralism of beliefs, methods, and pathways is honored
> without considering this to be a threat to any one pursuit.

Frequent and rapid historical change is recognized as a
benefit, while we preserve a degree of continuity in norma-
tive principles.[17]

The bottom line is that the individual is increasingly encouraged in
the use of his full potential; and at the same time, the need is to
broaden the spheres of space and time of which the individual
must be conscious.

A new spirit is everywhere, prompting local initiative,
broader participation by all, and a reexamination of older authoritarian policies. New participatory relationships are being established between labor and management, - for example, in the
revolutionary Saturn plant of General Motors. The critical examination of nuclear deterrence and the capitalist economics, by the
U.S. Catholic bishops, has been done for the first time by
extensive consultation with very many disparate groups, greatly
involving the Catholic laity and persons from other faiths. (It's
widely recognized that the methods thus developed will be of
even greater importance than the positions thus tentatively
reached.) New collegial relationships between lay people and
clergy are being established in the tens of thousands of 'base
communities' of South America. This development is matched by
new liberating theologies and new emphasis on the needs of local
cultures in South America, Africa, and Asia. Many more voices
are being heard.

Society, including the churches, has a very long way to go,
but at least there is significant movement towards more participa-
tive styles of authority. With sufficient awakening, we can reasonably hope that the concepts of participatory management, participatory politics, and participatory economics, all will continue to
evolve.

It would seem to be of the utmost importance, for both the
development of more effective institutions, and the development
of the human potential, that this movement be encouraged. We
can expect this partially through the increasing awareness of many
persons, but more practically because it's good for all parties in the
long run. Broad participation is good business because it actually
increases productivity, quality, and profits. It's good for every
organization - industrial, social, or religious - because it grows the
participants who contribute to that organization. Personal health,
based on a sense of accomplishment and self worth, improves. A
healthier world and greater personal fulfillment for its inhabitants

should result. Thus, in the area of authority, (as well as in the areas of money and sex), the fundamental option of growth of consciousness makes sense.

4.6 ILLUSIONS

Total awareness of reality is not as common as one might think. For example, it seems that many of us have some illusions of omnipotence, and need to work at avoiding them. People subconsciously say: "Smoking doesn't bother me, - I'll get away with it;" or "Others have to work hard to get somewhere, but it really should come easier for me;" or "I'm healthy, so I can eat anything without serious harm;" or "I'm independent and self-sufficient, so I don't need friends." People who acquire a position of authority and power, too, often get to feel that they are somehow above other humans, and possess some unique and indispensable gifts. In these and countless other ways we may avoid reality, ignore our limitations, and live in a narrow, imaginary world.

When we don't see the grandeur of the space and time about us, we can also become obsessed with minute problems and irritations. That may cause us to create an illusion of another kind. We may, for example, feel that people somehow do not value us enough, or are not considerate enough in how they treat us. We can readily create and then subconsciously maintain an exaggerated sense of our own inadequacy. In that illusory and defensive state, we may feel like striking back by finding fault with everyone and everything. People thus may fill their lives with objections; they may only think themselves vindicated when they find an objection to something. Much energy is thus wasted on small things that may be wrong, rather than recognizing the really big things that are wrong, and trying to do something about them.

We actually allow such illusions to develop. They then imprison us and act as impediments to full consciousness. Like living a lie, the illusion eventually becomes a heavy burden. Stress and anxiety can result. Our lives are strained to preserve the pretense. Finally, we have to face the reality of ourselves, as we stand back and see ourselves enmeshed. Part of human capability is to so observe ourselves and resolve to change. The creative process that we share in involves stripping away the encrustations we may have willingly accumulated. We must "die to ourselves" as necessary to get our freedom once again.

A great weapon against illusions of omnipotence, inadequacy, or persecution is genuine humility that involves broad
awareness. The truly humble person recognizes that we are all
part of the same grand creation, - earth and all minerals, plants,
and living creatures on it. We recognize our kinship with all of
creation, and particularly with all human beings, spread over all
space and time. We accept the fact that a loving parent-God
created us as we are, and we are thus destined to 'grow where
we're planted' and to build upon what we've been given. Then, in
this broad view, we are more likely to respect all as a grand gift
wherein we each are privileged to play a very respectable role.
Even our emotions and passions, our more 'earthy' properties, are
seen as blessings in that grand design. Then, in a healthy awe and
appreciation of the vast gifts in all of creation, we see our common
grandeur as well as our common frailties. With that immense and
beautiful view, we are less likely to arrogantly try to dominate that
universe. An illusion of omnipotence appears to be more and
more ridiculous. We are also less likely to feel we are an inferior,
oppressed part of it, but rather a vital element of something very
wonderful.

With great relief, we get back our freedom when we abandon
the illusion. Sam Keen writes: "Once we are able to confess that
we are not the center of the world, we perceive things in an
altogether new way. We are set free to admire rather than possess,
to enjoy rather than exploit, to accept rather than grasp. In the
attitude of wonder, we experience life as a gift".[18] Our precious
life is seen to be truly fragile and worthy of great care.

Thus, the higher levels of consciousness have another related
function, - that of examining ourselves objectively, and then
cleansing ourselves of illusions that we erroneously allowed
ourselves to be taught earlier. Getting rid of that nonsense sets us
free to live more fully in the real world.

4.7 INTEGRATION AND MULTI-LEVEL HARMONY

A frequent phenomenon is that pressures in our lives tend to
fracture our personalities, so we become almost different persons
in different circumstances. Some ability to adapt, of course, is
good. For example, when at work or play, on the job or at home,
with friends or foes, different sets of ·resources are needed.

However, to keep ourselves whole, we need to preserve a degree of consistency in all that we do. This is especially true in regard to money, sex, authority, and many other activities that can be either gems or obstacles. We need to avoid the inclination to operate in a separate world, with 'abnormal behavior', contrary to our fundamental option, where they are involved.

In ordinary living, we encounter situations where it is tempting to operate purely selfishly or with unbridled emotions. The dangers of entrapment are admittedly real, and should not be ignored. However, escape from these dangerous situations may not be possible or even desirable. On the one hand, satisfying purely selfish desires seems to result in a progressive corrosion of consciousness. On the other hand, great good can sometimes result from a proper use of these energies. Furthermore, self denial of that satisfaction, or reserving that satisfaction to appropriate circumstances, strengthens will power and further establishes the identity of the person. We must live in somewhat dangerous circumstances and struggle to preserve our integrity. As we find ourselves being separated from our set course, we need to constantly reconstruct ourselves to keep our personality whole.

The ideal for most people, then, would seem to lie in an integration of all aspects of our being, including our emotions and passions, and in the wise use of these gifts in full consciousness of others. The objective seems to be the concurrent use of our higher and lower levels of consciousness, with the "adult" in us affecting the "child" as necessary. Experience indicates that to counter the tendency to a fractured personality, things like money, sex, and authority are best approached with the adult objective of maximizing the good in the larger spheres of space and time.

A relevant analogy, we think, is in the area of photography. We can take a picture where only the close-in object is in focus, and the broader background is completely blurred. Conversely, with the right camera settings, we can achieve a greater depth of focus, and have a picture where the beauty of the background is also in focus. Similarly, then, if the focus is only on the accumulation of money, or the exercise of power, or the mechanics of the sex act, there can be a lack of focus on the broader and higher level of reality. But, with a little care, we can keep our higher purposes in mind, also.

The thing that keeps our entire picture in focus, and prevents fissures from happening, can be a simple philosophy or set of principles we can hang onto, in every circumstance. We suggest that this can be an emphasis on empathy and a deliberate awareness of the Divine Providence. These effectively stimulate a broad consciousness in space and time. If, in the midst of the financial deal, or the direction of subordinates, or the intimacies of sex, or the management of projects, we can consider the feelings of others, and also ponder a dialog with God and openly seek his way, then it would seem that consciousness is thriving. In each experience, we must deliberately fight our way out of a narrow fixation; then that victory leaves us with a renewed sense of purpose and personal satisfaction. Perhaps only in this way can we grow.

For a full harmony among all our levels of consciousness, it seems that we must strive to keep in mind a certain clarity of purpose at the higher levels. For example, we can be mindful of ourselves as participants in God's on-going creation. This must remain, to some degree, in focus, and become dominant when necessary, even when we are experiencing the semi-autonomous lower levels of conscious activity. We can strive to orchestrate all parts of our being, looking on them as our allies. We can steer them into harmony with empathy, caring love, and kindness, and thus keep our entire being in harmony with the Divine plan.

We intuitively feel, in doing all this, that we "preserve our integrity"; we stay whole. This is essential to the growth of our own image of ourselves, and our feelings of self worth and dignity. Keeping that harmony with the best our 'Adult' mind can perceive, and staying open to the inspiration of our inner light, of God whispering to us, brings peace of mind. Then we're no longer at war with ourselves; we function more smoothly; our joy is fresh like a breeze, and our satisfaction is sure and tranquil. In this way, though perhaps only in small steps, we each effect both our own development and the growth of consciousness in the world around us. Every challenge, then, is in reality an opportunity to respond to our inner self, and hence to further the growth of the spirit of God within us.

REFERENCES

[1] P. D. Ouspensky, *The Fourth Way*, Vintage Books, New York, 1971, p. 365.

[2]Teilhard De Chardin, *Building the Earth*, Avon Books, N.Y., N.Y., 1969, p. 78.

[3]Andrew Greeley and Mary Greeley Durkin, *How to Save the Catholic Church*, Viking Penguin Inc., New York, 1984, p. 43.

[4]James Gaffney, "Marriage and Family: Between Traditions and Trends", *Questions of Special Urgency*, Georgetown University Press, Washington, D.C., 1986, p. 15.

[5]Rabbi William B. Silverman, *The Jewish Concept of Man*, B'nai B'rith Youth Organization, Wahington, D.C., 1976. p. 24.

[6]Ellen K. Coughlin, "Dissenting Catholic Theologian Preaches a More Critical Approach to Moral Issues", *The Chronicle of Higher Education*, June 24, 1987.

[7]Andrew Greeley and Mary Greeley Durkin, *loc. cit.*, p. 68.

[8]Leonardo Boff, *Church: Charism & Power*, Crossroad, New York, 1985, p. 43.

[9]Harlan Cleveland, "The Twilight of Hierarchy", *Information Technologies and Social Transformation* National Academy Press, Washington, D.C., 1985, p. 61.

[10]Chester Barnard, *The Functions of the Executive*, Harvard University Press, Cambridge, 1938.

[11]William Ouchi, *Theory Z*, Addison Wesley Publishing Co., 1981.

[12]Leonardo Boff, *loc. cit.*, pp. 32–46.

[13]James C. Livingston, *Modern Christian Thought*, Macmillan Publishing Co., New York, 1971, p. 487.

[14]Bernard Haring, "Moral Theologian Under Attack: Saint Alphonsus Liguori", *America*, May 2, 1987, pp. 363–366.

[15]Gustavo Gutierrez, *A Theology of Liberation*, Orbis Books, Maryknoll, N.Y., 1973, p. 10.

[16]William D. Dinges, "The Vatican Report on Sects, Cults, and New Religious Movements", *America*, September 27, 1986, p. 147.

[17]John Langan, "Political Hopes and Political Tasks", *Questions of Special Urgency*, J.A.Dwyer, Editor, Georgetown University Press, Washington, D.C., 1986, p. 117.

[18]Sam Keen, "Hope in a Posthuman Era", *The Christian Century*, Jan.25, 1967

5

RESHAPING SOCIETY

The growth of consciousness in individuals must be reflected in the civilizations they produce. A look at the past and present societies indicates that the struggle for the birth of a greater worldwide consciousness is difficult indeed, and puts large responsibilities on each of us.

5.1 RETROGRESSIONS

Though we remain optimistic about the long term growth of consciousness in the world, we all know from bitter experience that in the short term there are violent swings in this commodity. Persons, communities, and nations all are subject to painful retrogressions. The frequent subordination of ethical norms to expediency, convenience, and profits, can gradually turn persons and the nation into dens of thieves and liars at home, while internationally transforming us into just another gang of bullies menacing the planetary village.[1]

The awful recollections of the relatively recent Nazi madness prove the point. In the lust for power by that government, the dignity of persons was denied; people were declared to be inferior and unworthy of respect or empathy; uncounted thousands died by callous cruelty and execution.[2] Nine to ten million Slavs were executed. Nearly 4.5 million Jews died in the gas chambers. In the first campaign of "depolanization", 1.2 million non-Jews and 300,000 Jews were exiled; nearly one third died of freezing, malnutrition and asphyxiation. It's estimated that in Ukrainia and Belorussia the Holocaust claimed 4.3 million non-Jews and a 1.25 million Jews. Nor was this the only such catastrophe in our life times. The 'fields of blood' in Cambodia also marked a high in the inhuman treatment of millions who died piteously at the hands of ruthless ideologues. The good news is that now such events have a tremendous impact on the world-wide conscience. Modern communications aid in the awareness of the injustices being done; more often than not, the world consciousness can and does prevent such catastrophes. Each one of us contributes in some way to the climate of society, making such excesses more or less controlled.

Those who lived or died in those depressions could not see the end of those terrible times, but those times did end. We owe it to those people and to ourselves to remember their suffering. Yes, such madness is still possible, and requires eternal vigilance to prevent its recurrence. These are real survival challenges; through it all, humankind needs to still see the possibility of a positive direction, and the roles that growth in consciousness can play, in the long term. We need to dedicate our entire personhood to that growth process, so that progress continues without the violent retrogressions we have witnessed.

5.2 INFLUENCE OF CULTURE

One would think that the fabulous cultural inheritance which is reflected in most societies and in all of our major religions should have enabled us to avoid the personal and national calamities noted above. On the other hand, we also know that there is an inclination to sometimes distrust our inheritance and to act impulsively, as we discussed earlier. The 1960's, for example, were a time when most authority systems were held by many to be obsolete and unworthy. Thus there is a tension between benefitting from our cultural inheritance and distrusting it. Where and how is the proper balance to be found? What is our culture, anyway?

By culture we mean everything we have learned, and have been taught, by our environment, by those around us, and by institutions we know. We may draw this culture from all those that went before us in all parts of the world. Sadly, on the other hand, we may be in ignorance of all that heritage, and we may settle for the street culture of the demagog or gang leader, whose exploits we admire and whose beliefs we therefore adopt. Whatever it is, this culture obviously can play a major role in influencing our lives; culture does permeate and affect every level of our consciousness. Every intuition, impulse, opinion, and fear is influenced. Therefore, our culture must be examined carefully and not followed blindly. Our broad inherited culture contains much that is valuable and essential to our current society; however, every culture must be made subordinate to our own highest level of consciousness, if that level is to determine our way of life.

It may help to try to understand how and from where our culture has come to us. Long past cultures, it seems doggedly leave their residue in present day institutions. For example, when the emperor, Constantine, made Christianity the religion of the empire, a fusion of cultures took place. Some present emphasis on Roman-like law and hierarchical authority owes much to the structure of Roman civilization. Philosophy and doctrine, too, draw insight from different cultures; and these may persist tenaciously also. Augustine reportedly melded selections from Manichaeism, a philosophy of Arabic origins, with those of the Roman church. St. Thomas Aquinas studied Aristotle (a 'pagan' philosopher) through the writings of Moses Maimonides (a Jew) and Averroes and Avicenna (Arabian philosophers). Thus, threads of cultural concepts from very different times and places have been woven into our heritage. The original views may today be difficult to uncover.

Sometimes culture is preserved simply as accumulated wisdom which we can examine and selectively adopt. Other times, however, it is presented more forcefully as "this is the way we do things." Further, to enforce the standards, the supposed wisdom is sometimes expressed in terms of regulations or laws for the community. This is understandable, because without strong traditions or laws societies have disintegrated in chaos. Thus do sets of laws evolve. Notable as early law givers were the Babylonians, Egyptians, Hebrews, Greeks, Romans, and the early English. A close intertwining of societal laws with religious practice was seen in the Jewish, Hindu, and Muslim cultures. These laws serve to establish and clarify the aspirations of the community. They provide a stability, on the one hand; but they may also inhibit the acceptance of new insights and the meeting of changing needs. Their enforcement tends to set things in concrete and inhibit further growth and adaptation. Fear of punishment can become the primary mechanism rather than conscious and free decision making. When there is insufficient opportunity for assessment and voluntary adoption of a culture, the result can be a reduction of personal consciousness, replacing it with only a dutiful compliance. Then, a negative reaction to those who enforce the culture, and to the content of the culture itself, can be expected.

Different groups, such as the churches and schools of philosophy, attempt to express a consensus of their communities. Some few things are held to be fundamental and more certain, and we can benefit greatly from that considered judgement. Many other things are clearly in the early stages of the search for understanding, and the consensus on these matters is still fluid. Institutional propositions on the latter still merit our respect,[3] but hardly our rapid assent. Rather, we are all participants in that searching process, and have a responsibility to contribute to it. Recognition of this spectrum of understanding, calling for various degrees of appreciation, is necessary if we are to benefit from accumulated wisdom and also avoid foolish and dogmatic upgrading of early speculations.

One of the areas of great cultural change today is that of sexuality. Many persons are distressed by the rapidity of that change and are convinced of its harm. Few however, would support the concepts of much earlier times, reflected in the reported view of Pope St. Gregory the Great. It was a doctrine supposedly propounded by him: "It is as impossible to have marital intercourse without sin as to fall into the fire and not burn."[4] Most persons today would see that view as one lacking in fundamental understanding, out of touch with reality, and a victim of a misled isolated culture. Subsequently, there have been efforts to describe a positive theology of the use of our God-given gift of sexuality.

Thus, we can understand that even honest desires to preserve or build human dignity in a given culture may produce conclusions which are seen to be very lacking in understanding later on. To guard against such blind alleys, we need improved ways of sharing one another's experience and inspiration, ways of developing consensus, and ways of reflecting that consensus in the more formal expressions of our culture. This task is never finished. A growing consciousness requires frequent reassessments with associated attempts to arrive at new consensus.

Evidently, inherited culture can be confining, - even imprisoning. It must be analyzed critically from time to time, and purified with determination. On the other hand, it also contains the essential gems of past understanding handed on to us. The evolving culture is a vital part of the whole evolutionary process, affecting us and all future generations. It is one of the ways in which real advances in consciousness can be passed on to future generations. Our inherited culture therefore must be approached empathetically and respectfully. Then, we can and must grow with it, and make our own small contributions to the evolving culture. It becomes a dynamic part of our equipment which can help to avoid catastrophes in our lives and in our world.

This cultural inheritance of ours is exceedingly valuable - indeed, priceless. We simply have to recognize its nature, if we are to really understand what parts are valuable, to make effective use of them, and to set aside some others. If we understand the source, then the value is there even though much has been formulated from a particular vantage point, which may have been quite myopic. In each different viewpoint, we very often can find underlying elements of great value.

In doing this, a deep respect for earlier thinkers is often in order, even when we now disagree with them. Profound truths are often only partially perceived. Brave people attempt to express that perception, and usually must do so within the limits of their poor language and the limited concepts of their own culture. The expression may thereby be flawed, even though the underlying perception may be on the right track. Accordingly, critical reflection on the inheritance from past cultures may not be so much in opposition to them, as it is an attempt to understand the past circumstances. This then permits a search for the underlying principles or hidden gem of wisdom that may be there, and may still be applicable in some form today.

Everyone can consider himself to be part of the on-going development of culture. The challenge to penetrate, with deeper insights, to an understanding of life, values, and future directions is given to all. Everyone has the opportunity of contributing to cultural development within the realm of family and friends. This, then may extend outward to others. The marriage of inherited discernmentsts with newer insights is thus a constant, universal, on-going process. It is a reflection of the growing consciousness of millions of participants in the evolving society.

5.3 SEPARATISM

Consciousness involves a sense of comradeship with all others. That tends to bring harmony to our lives. Things that separate us, one from another, and group from group, create stress, neurosis, and even violence. Sometimes the things we think are constructive, because they start out that way, take a turn towards being separatist and destructive, instead. The consequences can be a deep victimization and impoverishment of groups through cultural disparagement. Three examples of this are elitism, the notion of 'chosen people', and dogmatism. In each case, we need to understand the phenomena, and work to counter the harmful effects by promoting broader consciousness.

Elitism

One of the very common occurrences, that restricts the spheres of consciousness is the notion that we are somehow a member of an elite group, to the exclusion of others. Elitism often starts in a well-intentioned way, to promote the preservation of important values, or to resist the contamination of values from outside pressures. It can quickly result, however, in the failure to extend empathy outside the elite. It can foster the unwarranted belief that those outside the elite are somehow not as human and not as worthy of respect. The final elitism would seem to be the belief that those on the outside are not as fully loved by God.

Stereotyping fosters elitism and discrimination. Everyone in a certain group, we carelessly say, has some (usually negative) characteristics. Thus, we put people in a small box of our own creation. Every ethnic, racial, and religious group, - for example, Italians, Irish, Germans, Blacks, Jews, and Catholics, are prey. People stereotype others to give themselves a comfortable feeling of superiority or security. Stereotyping may even intimidate the victims sufficiently to give a measure of control over them. Once it is popular to intimidate, it becomes a matter of cowardice not to go along with the 'fun'.

Stereotyping an individual often results from sloppy thinking and a willingness to draw broad conclusions from partial information. Every one of us can be slandered totally if someone takes true scraps of information from our past lives and presents them one-sidedly, out of context. We often have good reason to be suspicious of others; but negative judgements based on such partial information are best labeled clearly as tentative. If we are aware that they are not well founded, we can act differently than if we gullibly accept the half-baked conclusion fully.

A historical example of elitism is found in the Hindus, who were divided into several thousand castes, which separated people socially and economically. These boundaries could not be crossed. The order of the principal castes was: 1) priests, 2) soldiers and administrators, 3) merchants and farmers, and 4) laborers and servants. One's daily life was different, depending on which caste one was in. The entire system bred intolerance and oppression. The priestly caste presumed itself to be a 'master people', loved by God. The others were not so chosen.

For centuries, the Jews were falsely stereotyped, and hated. Fortunately, that has been greatly reduced. Today, however, there are new hatreds, fanned by stereotyping. Studies of Arab stereotypes, in Hebrew children's books, are disconcerting.[5] El Asmar notes, "The young reader is educated through this literature to avoid the Arabs. He or she is warned not to approach the Arabs because they are physically filthy and diseased, because they steal, because they cannot be trusted, because they swear constantly, and because they are corrupt."[6]

Elitism is seldom acceptable, because it fundamentally narrows consciousness and dehumanizes the others. It must, therefore be fought, but fought with understanding of how it comes about, of the needs of the perpetrators for an unwinding of inherited prejudices, and for their gradual growth in consciousness.

In almost every case, one can discern the same sickness, the narrowing of the spheres of consciousness. The consequences are often intolerance, injustice, and the resulting reactions of hatred and violence. The antidote is the same: to work unceasingly to extend, in space and time, the individual and then the collective consciousness.

Chosen Ones

One of the serious elitist-related confusions surrounds the notion of being a 'chosen people', with some special role to play, through God's design. There seems to be some truth to this. How can we reconcile this with the broader view of God's love for all, and the fulfillment of all persons in his plan?

There are many current examples where economic interests, the desire for tribal cohesiveness, or various forms of selfishness cause groups to separate themselves from others. Those 'in the group' may give preferential treatment to those within their group, may mistreat others, and, in short, may close down empathy for those outside their group. It is very easy for them to substitute their plan for God's plan, and to assume that their purpose must be God's purpose. Sometimes, their purpose is, in reality, contrary to God's, despite their illusion of the opposite. Many crimes are all too often covered over by the otherwise good sense of being 'called' by God. One example will suffice. The Dutch Reformed theologian Carel Boshoff, in defending the practice of apartheid, in South Africa, said recently:

> We reject integration in all forms. The Afrikaner people were called into being by God and throughout our tortuous history we see his helping hand. Time and time again, he has reassured us and brought us back to our destiny, which is to fulfill our calling in South Africa as white people.[7]

We can easily reject such self serving assumptions of God's favor. And yet, we all do feel 'called' to serve. There is something to this notion of being chosen.

We described in chapter 3 the hypothesis that there is an 'action of God', - a spark, so to speak, in each of us, urging us to true fulfillment in accord with God's plan. We have the ability to respond affirmatively, but we can choose to respond to this 'holy spirit', or not, and to varying degrees. All such responses more or less affect those around us, and hence affect the culture of our time and place. Thus, every one of us has a calling to respond; and everyone of us makes some contribution, positive or negative, to our culture.

Each of us is 'chosen' to play a role in the evolution of consciousness, but we may choose to ignore that calling. Like-wise, by the aggregate of its members, each community and nation has an opportunity to respond, and thus has a potential role. Some very positive responses will have significant long-term effects on the growth of consciousness, and will render great service to others. This, of course, depends in part on the opportune circumstances in which these persons or groups find themselves, as well as on their superior response.

Certain of these responses by individuals, communities, and nations, have made an historical contribution, and are rightly celebrated. They responded well to their opportunities. Most of the world's religions, and many heroic persons in history can similarly be celebrated as outstanding examples of positive response to God's urgings towards higher consciousness.

Though usually less acclaimed, it seems reasonable to hold that the Holy Spirit acts similarly in all persons and all cultures. Everyone is part of a 'chosen people' because all persons have some unique opportunities to contribute, and each is 'chosen' for some role in the evolution of consciousness. Each of us is inclined to "grow where we're planted," to make the most of our given opportunities to serve and to fulfill our potential. As we do, we get great satisfaction from an awareness of the part we play, and of the contribution we make, however large or small.

Thus, we are all chosen to serve in the work of increasing world consciousness. Those who have contributed much to this work are justly celebrated. However, the exaltation of one group over another by the claim of a preferential chosenness by our common God can only lead to separatism and a loss of consciousness. Obviously, we need a broader consciousness, which includes all peoples, to clarify the fact that the only true 'chosenness' is being chosen to serve, and that service to humankind knows no boundaries of any kind.

Dogmatism

Learned groups, down through the ages, have tried to focus on fundamental truths that can provide a basis for their lives or their beliefs. This may be a political, sociological, philosophical, religious, or ideological set. Who could object to such a worthy cause? Problems may develop, however, if these opinions are allowed to breed separatism, because of unnecessary implications of enmity or inferiority of the others, who may not similarly promote these truths. These ego-building implications can lead to antagonisms and hatred.

We see this frequently in dogmatic antagonists, whether of
the political, ideological, or religious variety. Their view tends to
narrow to their selected fundamentals, (such as anti-communism
in politics or biblical interpretation in religion), while more important concepts (such as justice or empathy), which should be
considered more fundamental, are neglected. First there may be
the unwarranted and even arrogant presumption of superior
knowledge and absolute certitude about some set of 'truths' or
principles. Then comes the resistance to new insights on these
fundamentals, and a messianic conviction that these principles, as
understood by them, absolutely must be applied in all situations.
Or, it may simply be an unhealthy overemphasis on the importance of the fundamentals selected, and an unwarranted denunciation of those who do not share the same convictions.

Soon there are opponents to that claim of certitude, who are
then self-righteously classed as enemies of the fundamental truth.
The world is thus gradually polarized, divided into only two
classes, the 'good guys' and the 'bad guys'. Everything is seen in
black or white; "you're either totally with us or totally against us,"
and there is no other way. Of this was born the religious wars of
the Middle Ages, Mc Carthyism of the 1950's, and the 'evil empire'
concepts of today.

Arnold observes, concerning the related phenomena of dogmatic fundamentalism: "(It) is a historically recurring tendency
within Judeo-Christian-Muslim religious traditions that regularly
erupts in reaction to cultural change... (Dogmatic) fundamentalism at root feeds on fear and anger and, in many ways, provides
opportunities for revenge upon agents of change."[8]

We need to recognize dogmatism and dogmatic fundamentalism for what they are, and work to escape their entrapments, to
which we are all subject. We need to accept the element of
uncertainty in all of our knowledge, and to try to understand the
merits of the different viewpoints of others. This involves pulling
ourselves out of the emotional addiction to our own established
positions. It means using our higher levels of consciousness to see
the broader view, in a spirit of caring for others, instead of simply
being mechanically defensive and preserving a false sense of
righteousness. We need to remind ourselves of the God-given
dignity of others and the respect their views may deserve. Like it
or not, we have to constantly broaden our view, see the issue from
the other person's viewpoint, and seriously try to discern if there
is some wisdom there.

Acceptance

All forms of separatism persist. However, there have been major developments to encourage us in the belief that progress in their eradication is possible. The Enlightenment period, from 1648 to the French Revolution, was one of the significant steps in the growth of consciousness in the West. The Enlightenment marked the emergence of individual reason and conscience as the primary arbiter of truth and action. For the people of the Enlightenment, the great enemy was the presumed omniscience of dogmatic authoritarianism and its associated intolerance. As a result, it fostered the idea that rights and obligations are centered in individuals, rather than only in groups. When followed, these concepts tend to promote respect for the individual; and that basic respect tends to oppose elitism, discriminatory chosenness, and dogmatism. Rugged individualism, of course, also has its problems. Further progress is made as improved means of communication facilitate the sharing of experience and the arrival at consensus.

Evidently, we are still working on the fruition of these ideas; but their permeation of society has gradually encouraged a practical acceptance of persons who are different from those who dominate a given group. Bossman defines this practice:

> Acceptance among different people implies acknowledging the right of the other to exist and be what he or she is. It does not imply changing. Neither does it imply inadequacy or lower standing. Rather, acceptance implies a willingness to seek further understanding in the interest of personal growth in knowing and appreciating what is different. In this environment, the differing person is not viewed as deviant, but simply as other.[9]

Such acceptance does not adopt what is considered to be evil, but it does strive to understand the reasons for differences in culture, practices, and beliefs. Acceptance thrives on a fuller consciousness, involving empathy, caring love, and kindness, despite great differences. That growing consciousness gradually fosters the necessary mutual respect and basic equality which is essential for a world full of amazing and productive diversity. Evidences of such growing acceptance are the major efforts made during the last twenty years at rapprochement among different religious

groups, - particularly among diverse Christian groups, and between Christians and Jews.[10] Lesser but also significant steps have
been made by Christians towards understanding the Muslims and
Far Eastern religious groups.

A wider consciousness, that recognizes the humanity in the
'other camp', has gradually spread from those seeds that were
well watered in the Enlightenment. Each generation tries to give it
new life. In its current form, Glenn Tinder called it the 'new
civility'.[11] As D.Sturm recently construed it:

> First, it affirms that each individual and every community
> may be possessed of some important truth about the human
> condition. There is no absolutely 'evil empire'.

> Second, it sustains a posture of openness, even toward
> perceived enemies. It is always prepared to hear the other
> side and to correct its ways. It is self critical.

> Third, it acknowledges the kinship of all humanity, even all
> being. Thus, it rejects the principle of dipolarity, and works
> steadily and aggressively toward forming institutions of
> conciliation and mutual enhancement.[12]

We each play a role in this further 'enlightenment' that promotes
acceptance. Those of us with a remaining tendency to separatism
usually learn, eventually, that this 'new civility' (based on increased empathy and tolerance) leads to greater understanding,
appreciation, peace of mind, and old-fashioned enjoyment of life.

5.4 SOCIAL INJUSTICE

The term 'social justice' sometimes brings to mind the concept of
entitlement. We are entitled to some things, we think, and it is an
injustice if we are deprived of them. We are inclined to ask, then,
"To what are we entitled?" And, "Who owes it to us?" Following
the previous line of reasoning, though, we want to suggest that
we are all primarily entitled, by God's plan, to the opportunity to
grow towards full personhood, with expanded consciousness. In
participating in that plan, we must exercise empathy to help

others achieve that same fulfillment. Everything else must be subordinate to this and supportive of it.

Psychologists tell us that the average person experiences a hierarchy of needs. First, there is the need for survival, - for food, clothing, and adequate shelter. Once these lower needs are met, one can more easily seek the satisfaction of higher needs, such as self esteem and respect from others. At higher levels, still, one finds satisfaction in benefiting others, even the larger community or mankind. This higher need to provide service to others can become dominant; sometimes, however, these higher levels of satisfaction are not developed because of a concentration on the urgent demands from more primitive levels which have not yet been fulfilled. Thus, social injustice, that prevents the basic satisfaction of primitive needs, may sometimes inhibit the further development of consciousness, and hence the personal satisfaction at higher levels.

Institutions, too, affect our ability to grow. Many institutions are a direct result of the consciousness, or lack of same, of the more influential citizens. Their misuse of wealth or authority, sometimes coupled with an indulgence in elitism, can easily cause a great deal of institutionalized social injustice. All too often, vast injustices become the norm. The social institutions are shaped, and then frozen. Customs, regulations, and laws become fashioned to accept the status quo which favors some 'in' group. Subjugation, exploitation, poverty, and terror all grow in the society like diverse forms of cancer, and are accepted for a long time as being normal. People unnecessarily die of hunger, are illiterate, are unaware they are being exploited, and even become unaware that they are truly capable persons. These injustices remain institutionalized until the rights of full personhood for all people are further appreciated, and the resolve to act with empathy for all becomes more pervasive.

The pursuit of justice has a strong base in many religious cultures. The prophets of Israel were vehement and uncompromising in their condemnation of the political evils of their era. They raised their voices and risked their lives "to demand righteousness for those exploited by injustice, to seek bread for the poor, housing for the homeless, and mercy for the widow, the orphan, the stranger, and the afflicted."[13] The early Christians, like others, felt that their new philosophy could change the world. They were committed to building the Kingdom of God on earth, - a place of justice, freedom, and love.

Now, more than ever, the essential need for social justice is recognized, and this is being incorporated into philosophical, political, and religious programs. Liberation theology, originating in South America, is a current expression of this, which links the liberating theme of both the Old and the New Testaments to social justice today. 'Conscientization' seeks to raise people's awareness of institutional violence and structural injustice in society. Gustavo Gutierrez writes of liberation theology:

> This is a theology which does not stop with reflecting on the world, but rather tries to be a part of the process through which the world is transformed. It is a theology which is open - in a protest against trampled human dignity, in the struggle against the plunder of the vast majority of people, in liberating love, and in the building of a new, just, fraternal society - to the gift of the Kingdom of God.[14]

In this theology, love is said to be the inspirational soul of justice, and the struggle for social justice is an essential element of the Christian life. Social injustices can, of course, also be found outside of South America, - indeed, throughout every culture, including our own. Significant contributions to this theology are being made from Africa and Asia as well as South America. Liberation theology, in fact, applies to every region.

Empathy for all persons, therefore, inevitably involves seeking their freedom from unjust cultures and institutions. We each cannot achieve full personhood, in this inter-related world, so long as our neighbors are oppressed by a lack of consciousness for them. If this evil is institutionalized, then compassion requires that we join in the efforts to reform those institutions. What can we do?

> We can advocate respect and equality for women, blacks, and other minorities.

> We can advocate the right of every person to opportunities for meaningful work, and the education it requires.

> We can protest against the neglect of the hungry and those without decent housing; we can protest the diversion of funds from aid for the poor to excessive armaments-spending and subsidies for the very rich.

We can support cooperation on global and environmental problems, and changes in trade policies which tend to exploit underdeveloped countries.

We can protest against our government's support of repressive and terroristic governments, and those that have institutionalized social injustice.

We can understand the social stresses that drive some to violence, and work to remove those stresses. We can demand fairness and true justice for all, and even the means for rehabilitation for those who violate our laws.

We used to hear: "That's somebody else's business, not mine." Today, we increasingly hear that social injustice is everybody's business. To a degree, all persons have a prophetic vocation. Everyone has the opportunity and the obligation to be the 'prophet' that interferes with the way things are going, when that way heaps injustices on any person or group. As Matthew Fox says: "What is more ugly than the oppression of a royal person, an image of God, a living, creative, brother or sister? And what is more beautiful than to awaken people to their own dignity, and to the rights that accompany such dignity?"[15] In such efforts, we not only contribute to the well-being of others; we also fulfill our own purpose in life, and our basic responsibility, - to advance the consciousness of ourselves and of the larger community.

5.5 SEXUAL DISCRIMINATION

Sexual discrimination has been so ingrained in our cultures, for so long, that many people don't recognize it as such. This is not surprising, as that's been the case for many, if not most, forms of discrimination. One only has to recall the acceptance of slavery, and the maintenance of slaves by 'the best families' and, reportedly, even on the farms of religious orders. The biblical injunction, "Slaves, obey your masters," may have been good advice, but for a long time it seldom was accompanied by the demands for the abolition of slavery (even though that would seem to be a basic message of the New Testament). In a somewhat similar vein, the injunction, "Wives, obey your husbands," may promote temporary domestic tranquility, but one needs to look further to insure that the female has an equal opportunity to grow as a full person.

Women are often taught the arts of being relatively helpless, powerless, and without influence, starting at an early age. With lower self-esteem, they are then more vulnerable to violence, especially wife-abuse. If such a woman encounters a disoriented or power-hungry male, he may sense these moods of passivity and low esteem, and may then launch an easy psychological or physical conquest.

Anyone who always carries a sense of constant danger and a sense of being put in a second-class position is likely to have a problem in growing. Each person deserves the opportunity to develop the gifts with which he or she has been endowed. Becoming a full person requires a sense of freedom, a sense of security, and to be treated as a respected individual. Too often, the female has not experienced this because of the prevailing cultural attitudes towards that sex.

Culturally, if the media and entertainment worlds are any indicators, women are considered primarily for their sex appeal. To focus entirely on that part of sexuality which is physical is to ignore the larger personality. Even to give primary attention to this aspect, rather than the larger capability, and particularly to give lower emphasis to the intellect, consciousness, and psychological strengths of women, often results in treating them as something of a subhuman. (The deformation of the woman's personality might well be compared with the deformation of her feet by the shoes that a sex-oriented culture imposes on her.)

The roots of sexual discrimination go very deep, have become a part of many institutions, and are woven throughout our own and other cultures. Considering women as subhuman, for example, was described in the Old Testament (Judges 19) in the grisly story where women were literally thrown to the human wolves in order to spare a man. Even the noted 'doctors' of the church succumbed to the blasphemy. Consider these writings:

> You are the devil's gateway. You are the unsealer of that forbidden tree. You are the first deserter of the divine law. You are she who persuaded him whom the Devil was not valiant enough to attack. You destroyed so easily God's image, man. On account of your desert, that is death, even the Son of God had to die.
>
> Tertullian, De Cultu Fem. 1,1

How then did the apostle tell us that the man is the image of God and therefore he is forbidden to cover his head, but that the woman is not so, and therefore she is commanded to cover hers? Unless, according to that which I have said already, when I was treating of the nature of the human mind, that the woman, together with her own husband, is the image of God, so that the whole substance may be one image, but when she is referred to separately in her quality as a helpmate, which regards the woman alone, then she is not the image of God as fully and completely as when the woman too is joined with him in one.

Augustine, D Trinitate, 12.7, 10

Woman is said to be a misbegotten male, as being a product outside the purpose of nature considered in the individual case, but not against the purpose of universal nature.

Thomas Aquinas, I, 99, 2 ad 1

The gravity of a sin depends on the species rather than on circumstances of that sin. Accordingly we must assert that, if we consider the condition attaching to these persons, the man's sin is the more grievous because he was more perfect than the woman.

Thomas Aquinas, II, II, 164, 4[16]

Today these concepts are seen not merely as incorrect, or poor theology, but as profoundly evil, for their consequences contribute to the mistreatment and growth stunting of half the earth's population. Women's liberation stands alongside black liberation, and third-world economic liberation. In all these cases, they are long overdue cleansings of our culture that we must yet go through. For some persons and institutions, the cleansing will be painful.

Today, for example, there are women who feel that the institutional churches are trapped in a spirit of elitism that excludes women in many ways, because of old stereotypes. This is becoming less acceptable as stereotypes of women fade in our culture. Some women, and some men, too, even want to assert the rights of women to the priesthood. However, they find that they fly in the face of another group of people who want to maintain religious forms as they are. These understandably feel safe and secure in their faith, under a certain regimen. The sense of unity that they all want is jeopardized by the emotion of confrontation. The problem, then, is to work to raise the levels of consciousness and so ultimately combat elitism and prejudice, without unduly raising the levels of antagonism which actually restrict consciousness. That this is not a new problem is illustrated by the penetrating poem by Edwin Markham, who said:

> He drew a circle that shut me out,
> Heretic, rebel, a thing to flout.
> But Love and I had the wit to win;
> We drew a circle that took him in.[17]

Basically then, the issue is the recognition of the female as a full person, particularly possessing the intellectual, compassionate, and spiritual components. However, the issue also extends to the deformation of society as a whole as a result of this imbalance. Lacking the full participation of the female contribution, society is more inclined to an excessive compulsiveness not only in sex but also in militarism and the associated exaggerations of machismo. The liberation of the women so as to promote full development and full use of their apparent consciousness can, we believe, have a profound effect on the quality of life in our society as a whole, and on progress for all of us.

Fortunately, the solution is elementary. It simply requires the treatment of every person, male or female, as a truly beloved child of God, born in God's image, with the capability for reflective thought, creativity, and growth in consciousness! Awareness of the full person and the full potential of each person is needed, rather than the narrow stereotypes we have been willing to settle for. Let's get on with it.

Despite the long history of put-downs, many women today recognize that their state is taught and not inherent. They therefore learn to be more appreciative of themselves, to recognize their own potential, and hence to become more self-confident, decisive, and assertive. At least in this country, and many others, a growing portion of the female population has begun to live as full persons; and the struggle to do so has given them advantageous perspective and strength. In this, too, they deserve everyone's support.

5.6 THE STRUGGLE FOR BIRTH

Reading this chapter could be somewhat disheartening. A person can be assaulted by a wide variety of seemingly malevolent societal realities, such as suffocating cultures, arrogant illusions of self-sufficiency and power, demeaning elitism, segregation by those presuming to be 'chosen', narrow minded dogmatism, economic exploitation, and, for a woman, dehumanizing chauvinism. Even without physical violence (of which there is also plenty), survival often seems to call for brute animal instincts of 'dog eat dog' and 'ask no quarter; give no quarter'. How, in this kind of a world, can we still hope for a society which exhibits growth in things like empathy, caring love, and kindness?

That such growth is nevertheless possible does seem remarkable; but the simple truth seems to be that this growth is the only hope of civilization to avoid the escalation of violence and chaos. Birthing is never easy; and this birthing of the consciousness of the peoples of the world is no exception. As we've discussed, however, every obstacle also presents options for progress, and there are grounds for much optimism.

In fact, people in various cultures have been reexamining their roots and have been becoming more clear on which aspects of their cultures they want to retain. Scientific methods of such analysis have greatly improved, and have been increasingly adopted, promising continued illumination. The vast improvements in communications and media coverage also give many more people an understanding of other cultures. Though this is still in an early stage, continued technological improvements will foster further understanding. Gradually, we appreciate our universal kinship with all of creation; gradually, we better understand the basic needs of peoples we once only thought of as strangers and adversaries.

The interdependence of peoples likewise becomes more apparent, along with the realization that cooperation and mutual benefit work better, in the long run, than domination. The idea of mutual benefit extends, too, into the realm of personal freedom. As more people become aware of their own growth potentials, they also realize that freedom for others to fulfill their potential is to the benefit of all. Even in the area of sexual discrimination, a much greater cognizance of the problem has resulted in the beginnings of women's liberation.

Thus, while there is a tremendous amount yet to be done, and the obstacles at times seem insurmountable, there are, in fact, a great number of hopeful signs. The inner urgings to greater consciousness remain in everyone and most people realize that their real satisfaction and joy are in that direction. It does seem that the average level of consciousness in the world is growing as we take advantage of the communication advances at our disposal. A sense of greater unity, bread for all the world, and a steady improvement in caring justice can be seen as future possibilities.

That progress in reshaping society depends, of course, on the corresponding birthing process in each one of us. Society matures as we each mature, as we each work for the treatment of every other person as a child of God. We each need to steadily campaign for dignity of all persons, born in God's image, each with that amazing capability for reflective thought, creativity, and the growth of the interior essence we call consciousness.

REFERENCES

[1]Eugene Hillman, "Doing Evil for a Good Cause", *America*, May 10, 1986, p. 379.

[2]William J. O'Malley, "The Gentile Holocaust", *America*, June 14, 1986, p. 492.

[3]Ladislas Orsy, "Reflections on the Text of a Canon", *America*, May 17, 1986, pp. 396–399.

[4]M. Farrell, quoting theologian Father Charles Curran, in "Mahoney, Curran debate dissent perimeter", *National Catholic Reporter*, Oct. 24, 1986, p. 20.

[5]Adir Cohen, *An Ugly Face in the Mirror: National Stereotypes In Hebrew Children's Literature*, (in Hebrew) Reshafim Publishing House, Tel Aviv, 1985.

[6]Fouzi El-Asmar, *Through the Hebrew Looking Glass: Arab Stereotypes in Children's Literature*, Zed Books, London, 1986, p. 80.

[7]C.J.Green, "South African Church Leaders Speak Out", *Christianity and Crisis*, 45 (18) Nov 11, 1985, pp. 440–444.

[8]Patrick M Arnold, S.J. "The Rise of Catholic Fundamentalism", *America*, April 11, 1987, pp. 297 - 300.

[9]David M. Bossman, "'Nostra Aetate' in Cultural Perspective", *America*, Feb. 8, 1986, pp. 89– 91.

[10]*loc. cit.*.

[11]G. Tinder, *Tolerance*, 1976.

[12]D. Sturm, "Reagan's New Fundamentalism", *Christianity and Crisis*, 1985, pp. 318– 320.

[13]Rabbi William B. Silverman, *The Jewish Concept of Man*, B'nai B'rith Youth Organization, Wahington, D.C., 1976, p. 22.

[14]Gustavo Gutierrez, *A Theology of Liberation*, Orbis Books, Maryknoll, N.Y., 1973, p. 15.

[15]Matthew Fox, *Original Blessing*, Bear & Co., Santa Fe, New Mexico, p. 90.

[16]Joanne Koenig, "A Woman's Reflections: Life as Wife, Mother, Missioner in Community", *Maryknoll Formation Journal*, Spring-Summer '84, p. 51.

[17]Edwin Markham, *Anthology of the World's Best Poems*, Wm. H. Wiser Co., New York, 1953, Vol. 1, p. 265.

6

THE GROWTH OF WISDOM

This world-wide movement of humanity, towards a greater consciousness, sometimes seems chaotic and unreal. For more than five thousand years of recorded history, men and women have been struggling to discern humankind's value, purpose, and destiny. Various religious movements have tried to focus on what truly matters and where we're going. However, even these well meaning religious groups have fought bitterly. In the face of so much conflict over such a long time among the institutional religions of the world, which claim to promote greater consciousness, can we see any progress in the development of wisdom? Can we find common ground and coalescence among these religions? Can we see their contribution to the growth and birthing which is taking place in the world? Can we, in fact, consider ourselves to be in comradeship with many of the great streams of thought that have developed around different religious viewpoints?

We believe that a look at these diverse streams does reveal a process of growing awareness and an enlarging emphasis on consciousness that is heart-warmingly common and strong. In fact, it appears that many of the diverse streams of thought build upon one another, influence one another, and jointly contribute to the growth of the ocean of thought in which we live and develop. The growth of consciousness in many thousands of individuals is

111

thus reflected in a corresponding growth in the religiously oriented societies that people fashion in different cultures.

6.1 UNITY IN DIVERSITY

There is an evolutionary aspect to the formation of the world religions. As soon as humankind became capable of reflective thought, men and women began to wonder from whence they came and what their destiny would be. Primitive peoples speculated on the terrors of nature and focused on the anger and the unpredictability of the powers of the universe. Yet, as far back as we can see, even in the hearts of early men and women, there was the idea of affection and help for one another, a notion that love was possible in an unpredictable world. It seems that as we look back, there always was the river of God's love flowing into humanity.

God has created us all in her image. She has put this spark of divine love in all of us. Our duty is to take what she has given us and to "increase it 50 fold or 100 fold." We can only create greater love from the earth process by giving of ourselves to others. As God put this spark of love in all of us, we all have this inner urging to somehow become something greater. We find that this urge to become, prompts us to practice empathy, caring love, and kindness. However, as men and women gather in community groups to further this becoming, due to their personalities, their cultural aspects, and the historical time that they come upon the scene, they evolve a somewhat different focus on basic concepts. They also create certain rituals and creeds that they feel will enable them to better accomplish the process of growth in consciousness.

God made us all somewhat different. God seems to love diversity. God made all the animals, and all of the animals aren't lions. We also have deer; we have bear cubs; we have amoeba. Look at the birds. They aren't all robins. There is this wonderful variety that God has put into his creation, and into humanity. This diversity is reflected in humankind's religious beliefs. We come from different cultures. Our genetic makeup is different. Our separate and distinct environments influence us in varying directions. Therefore we couldn't possibly be expected to have exactly the same religious inclinations or worship within the same forms and rituals comfortably. Lo and behold, we don't. Just look at us!

Look at the marvellous variations in the religions of the world! These interact with one another. Each influences the other. Portions break down, change, evolve, and grow more fully. The whole creative process draws on a potential to become more. In some sense, all are in communion, dedicated to a common purpose. In that sense, all are one!

In spite of our differences, we find that there is much in common in our diverse pursuits of divinity and of a fuller realization of the human potential. We associate godliness with peace, justice, freedom, and other forms of goodness. We call a man godly, if he is considerate, compassionate, and loving towards others, promotes their physical and spiritual well being, and acts justly. A godly society is one which fosters such growth in its citizens, cares for its minorities and disadvantaged, and dwells in harmony with other nations. These qualities are widely valued today and have even been found germinating in the earliest religions.

6.2 THE GREAT RIVER DELTA

For illustrative purposes, we compare God's plan for humankind and our evolutionary thrusts to fulfill this plan, to a river that flows through time until it reaches the ocean of eternity. Recalling that we all are made out of the same star dust, and that we are all vehicles for this plan of God, we might suggest that humanity is an important link in something that God is developing. Perhaps the God of love is employing us through her creative process to become a greater quantity of love. Like the river, we move towards unity with the sea that is our source and our destiny, to be once again in union with our God. We all participate in this process, both those of us who have created vast amounts of love, and those who have only created a little.

Just as the delta of a river often has many different channels that go into the sea, so there are many diverse routes to God. You go in your channel, and I go in mine, but we come from the same river, the same source, the same star dust, the same creating love. There are many different channels humanity uses to get close to God; we have the Hindu and the Buddhist channels and the Muslim channel; we have the Jewish and the Christian channels, and many, many minor channels. We must not forget the atheistic and agnostic channels that some humans take in their pursuit of fulfilled living. Keep in mind that atheists come from the same loving source as any of us, and create their own particular channels to flow back to the sea.

Every stream in this delta is in constant change. Streams deepen, seek broader avenues, take new paths. Streams interact, mix, merge, and part again. Parts of each stream become parts of other streams. Each philosophical school, represented by these streams, evolves gradually. Some principles acquire greater prominence, and some concepts are modified or replaced with ones that better match the currently perceived reality. Each people builds on the heritage they have, as they see it. Each seeks fresh insights, a broader view, an integration of all that has been perceived. Often, this is accompanied by a degree of protest against a certain portion of the heritage which is felt to be a possible diversion. All this continuous change (or clarification) in the content of philosophical and religious streams is part of the birthing process, with men and women playing a stronger and stronger role in that creation, in response to inner urgings. God oversees all her creation, and takes each stream through the delta, and eventually out to the 'ocean of omega'.

6.3 THE HOLY BOOKS

Over the centuries, there have been many thousands of 'experts' and many associated writings trying to tell us what it is that will bring us happiness, contentment, or lasting satisfaction. Philosophers attempt to identify values and meaning in our lives; they attempt to discern a pattern or grand plan to reality. Some include the possibility of a Divine Providence in this overall plan. They believe that they experience an awareness of what has 'really' happened, over time; a realization of what brings true happiness; a new perception of reality, or a clearer view of our purpose on earth and our relation to our creator. These subjects are of such importance that those who feel they have found new clues often feel strongly motivated to share them.

Such expressions have been passed from person to person and from generation to generation. In earlier days, this accumulated wisdom was conveyed by the practice of the times, - by songs, myths, and parables. These were celebrated, discussed, and argued about; they helped to raise people's awareness in important matters. As writing became more widespread, these same ideas were reflected in the writings of some thinkers and, more frequently, in the writings of the followers of outstanding philosophers. Various schools of religious thought, in particular, have collected these ideas of what makes life worth living, as well as theories on our relation to God. In time, there has been a build-up of accumulated concepts, which different persons or groups attempted to evaluate, weed out, and systematize. Periodically, out of all the candidates would come a subset that the authorities of the day deemed the best, the most valid, and the most inspired. Some ideas would be discarded.

Thus, it seems that our knowledge is like evolution itself, - some main stems grow, but there also are dead branches. The main stems gradually become stronger, and the distracting side stems fall away. One can see this evolution in the writings of the major religions of the world. New insights are added to a core of the inheritance; then useless appendages grow; and these are discarded by reformers who build anew on that expanded core. This process contributes greatly to the 'sea of thought' in which we live, - which Teilhard called the 'Noosphere'. It is the precious conceptual heritage of the past. It is the base on which each new person can build his or her individual consciousness. Each individual must search through this heritage, to draw further insights, clarifications, and perhaps corrections of earlier perceptions. In trying to do this, we find that there are common threads, often submerged, in many of the scriptures. In particular, one can find that all of the scriptures tell in different ways of the birth of God's spirit in humankind.

6.4 THE NEAR EAST RELIGIONS

Each of the three great religions, Judaism, Christianity, and Islam, originated in the Near-East (though it is also possible that they were influenced by cultural exchanges with India and the Far East). Each of these favors a somewhat different expression of the nature of God. Each takes the position that their expression is guided by the Divine Providence.

We can set aside the comforts of elitism and recognize the probable universality of Divine Providence. We can recognize the

limitations of our finite comprehension and our cultural suscepti-
bility. We can accept the fact that our models of the ultimate reality
are necessarily approximate even though useful. Then we might
be ready to accept the fact that all three religious expressions of
reality are in a sense valid. Each has a role to play in teaching
people how to lead more fulfilling lives and in bringing persons
closer to union with the ultimate reality. Each serves those
purposes well, for different peoples. Each helps to birth the Spirit
of God over the centuries. There are many paths up the mountain,
depending on from where people start.

Hebrew Scriptures

The Jewish scriptures were built up over many centuries. Some of
the stories, such as the deluge, are reported to have existed at least
as early as 3000-1500 BC, in the writings of the Accadians, in
Mesopotamia.[1] Wisdom scholar Roland Murphy sees a great
influence of Egyptian concepts on the Israeli wisdom literature,
particularly the concepts of justice, order, and the divinely established harmony between nature and society.[2] It is also reported
that the later Babylonians possessed legends of the deluge and the
tower of Babel, which were accepted in the Old Testament.
During the captivity in Babylon, about 600 B.C., it was particularly
important that the Jewish traditions be preserved and taught, so a
major effort was made to reorganize and systematize their writings. Also, about the year 150, after the Jews had been driven out
of Jerusalem, the rabbis again sifted through their writings and
solidified their 'canon' of scripture, discarding some that were
more recent or considered to be less important.

The somewhat different emphases of Abraham, Isaac, Jacob,
Moses, and the prophets were woven into a powerful set of
complementary views. The personality of God in these writings is
very often kindly and forgiving, sometimes legally judgmental,
sometimes vengeful, sometimes fearsome, usually loving, sometimes favoring individuals with wealth and health, sometimes
favoring nations in battle, and often the God of the poor and the
wretched. Some saw God as punitive and disciplinary, but the
strongest thread was that of a life-giving, liberating, and affirming
God. The Jews crystallized the concepts of one divine force that
willed their freedom, their well being, and their salvation. The
goodness and kindness of God became the overwhelming hope.

The Jews perceived clearly that nature was not an insurmountable obstacle to progress, that change in the social order was possible, and that justice could be sought and obtained with the blessing of their loving God. They accepted as their responsibility the improvement of the social order when they saw a disharmony between the current state of affairs and the will of their loving creator. They emphasized that the fire of God's love had to reside in each person's heart to carry out this responsibility. Reflecting this, the prophets became unsurpassed protesters and reformers of the moral, political, and social conditions of their times. In these uplifting concepts, the Jews found purpose in their lives and purpose for their nation.

Faithfulness to God's commandments became the primary criterion of their destiny as a nation, and so the theological lawyers became intimately entwined with the political administration of the nation. The importance of caring love for one's neighbor was clear enough, but there were other strong emphases on the importance of law and all the rituals that accompanied the law, which tended at times to overshadow the primacy of love. Nevertheless, it has been truly remarkable that, despite terrible calamities of bondage, destruction of their homeland, dispersion, pogroms, and the more recent holocaust, the Jewish people have preserved for thousands of years the concept of a loving Divine Providence that will ultimately bring them to fulfillment in union with God.

The Hebrew scriptures contain much allegory:- "the description of one thing under the image of another...the veiled presentation, in a figurative story, of a meaning metaphorically implied but not expressly stated".[3] In this, they often offer the possibility of double meanings. For example, one can see the analogous work of God in the transformation of the human being, as well as the transformation of the land, in Isaiah 41:18:

> I will make rivers well up on barren heights, and fountains in the midst of valleys; turn the wilderness into a lake, and dry ground into waterspring.

(Jesus later echoed this second meaning with the expression "The water that I shall give will turn into a spring inside him, welling up to eternal life" - John 4:14b.)

Current interpretations of scripture within the Jewish community emphasize the potential of humankind and the fact that humans are created in the spiritual image of God, "a little lower than the angels" (Psalm 8). Thus we have as the modern Jewish concept of Man:

> All Persons are sacred, regardless of race, creed, or social position, but little less than divine. Those who despise, exploit, or destroy man are despising, exploiting, and destroying a measure of divinity. Those who serve and exalt man are serving and exalting God.

> Man is endowed with a divine potential for beauty and holiness,... a sacred personality that is related to the universe and is part of the divine purpose, - guided and motivated by the spiritual image of God within.

> Because all men are sacred, they are entitled to equal opportunities, and none is entitled to special privilege.[4]

One has to admit that these concepts are often violated, even today. (One blind spot seems to have been the lack of official Israeli sensitivity for the plight of non-Jewish Palestinians.) Nevertheless, the goals cited above seem clearer than ever; the violations are more widely denounced; and the islands of progress are widespread.

The expectation of the coming 'Kingdom of God' is the idea of a future era when all people will practice the will of God. It was consistent with the needs of the earlier times (under Roman domination) to look for such an event under the leadership of a great king or military hero, a Messiah. That expectation of a future time of greater love and kindness remains today in the Jewish culture.

Today, the possibility of an evolutionary growth within the community, towards this end, is compatible with this hope. An essential part of the Messianic promise is this same birth of consciousness, - that is, empathy, caring love, and kindness, with its associated freedom and justice, in the hearts of all humankind. That promise is, we suggest, the progressive birth of the Spirit of God in the world, until that Spirit permeates the human community.

Christian Scriptures

The Christians built upon the Hebrew foundation. Shortly after the year 150, the Christians adopted almost the same set of books that the Jews had assembled, adding a few more to make up their 'Old-Testament'. (Later Protestant Bibles rejected some of these additions.) The New Testament then went through many group-ings of writings over the next two hundred years. Marcion appears to have conceived of the uniquely Christian holy scrip-tures. His canon had only one gospel (a distorted Luke) and ten Pauline letters (some of the latter were later declared to be written by followers of Paul). The gospel of Peter was used at Rhossos till the end of the second century (and later rejected). Then, a growing flood of gnostic-tending gospels (Mary Magdalene, Thomas, Philip, etc.), prompted a redefinition of the canon by Irenaeus. This canon included the four gospels and Acts. It wasn't until the fourth century that Hebrews was recognized in the west as Pauline (but later thought to be of uncertain origin).

The New Testament is a proclamation of the faith of the early Christians. It describes how Jesus lived, taught, and healed all kinds of physical, psychological, and spiritual ailments. It an-nounces the joyous belief that this man personified the character of God himself, and that this life is the holy model by which all persons can order their lives.

The Christian message vividly emphasized those threads of the Jewish traditions which placed caring love and forgiveness at the core of human relations. What the Greek's called 'agape love', - that is, respect for all and a willingness to sacrifice for the good of others, was made its cornerstone. The ardent and passionate words of Jesus caught the imagination of his followers: "Love your neighbor as yourself.", "Love your enemies, and bless those that curse you.", "Forgive seven times seventy times.", "Be perfect (whole) as your heavenly Father is perfect.", "My peace (joy) I leave with you." Jesus evidently loved people, and they loved him in return.

His teachings released people from the bondages of guilt and fear of death. His example swept away the preeminence of selfishness. Jesus' way of life emphasized understanding and compassion for others through agape love (the full giving of self for others). This and his focus on the concept of the all merciful and intimately loving Father, became the inspiration for the Christian movement. The seeds of process theology were set in the early church. The great apostle, Paul, described the maturing of creation, as the Christians seek to follow Jesus' example (Romans 8:22-23):

> From the beginning till now the entire creation, as we know, has been groaning in one great act of giving birth; and not only creation, but all of us who possess the first fruits of the Spirit, we too groan inwardly as we wait for our bodies to be set free.

Within the Christian community, diverse emphases were nurtured in different cultures. The Trappists emphasized closeness to God through contemplation and isolation from worldly desire. The Franciscans emphasized a love of all creation, a sharing of poverty, and a love for the disadvantaged. Many societies of nuns emphasized community service and care for the poor and the sick.

The Eastern Orthodox community emphasized the role of the Holy Spirit acting through the minds of Christians as a whole. They tended to focus on the 'mind of Christ' acting through every person to influence the welfare of all of creation; they felt that God's truth is gradually discerned through a consensus of the 'conscience of the church'.[5]

In the sixteenth century, Luther, Calvin, King Henry VIII, and others started other Christian movements which rejected some rituals and contributed an emphasis on several theses which had grown somewhat dormant. The first thesis was that good works alone are insufficient; creeds and sacraments alone are insufficient. The key ingredients, it was stressed, are a faith which involves great love and trust, and an interior willingness to be an instrument of God's love. A second thesis was that great care has to be exercised lest we lose sight of the infinite God, who is beyond our symbols and rituals, and idolize our institutional processes. Less emphasis was placed on the assumption of static, inerrant knowledge, and the immutability of truth. More emphasis was placed on the continued unfolding of God's plan. More importance was also put on the direct action of the Holy Spirit in each person, often using Bible reading and group discussion as occasions for discerning the truth.

A great misconception is the belief that each of these movements has been in total and fundamental conflict with one another. Individuals have chosen to be in conflict; but to some extent each movement has been in search of harmony with the loving creator. To that extent, each movement provides another perspective, a portion of which adds to the total consciousness of our human race. In the end, all faiths benefit from the strivings for understanding done by each movement. In time, the best parts of each movement's insights can be quietly absorbed by the other faiths.

Muslim Scripture

Some 600 years after Christ, another movement, in a different culture, included parts of the earlier inheritance but set a somewhat different course suited to the needs of that time and place. The Qur'an, according to Muslim belief, was given by God through the lips of one man, Muhammad, and was written down at that time by his associates on bones and bark and leaves and scraps of parchment. It draws from the Arabian traditions, but it contains much material related to many of the subjects in the Old and the New Testaments (Qur'an 3:83):

> Say: We believe in Allah and that which was revealed to us, and that which was revealed to Abraham and Ishmael and Isaac and Jacob and the tribes and that which was given to Moses and Jesus and to the Prophets from their Lord; we make no distinction between any of them, and to Him we submit.

There are also sections particularly aimed at the rampant excesses of the then Arab world (licentiousness, degrading class distinctions, and commercialization of hundreds of gods).

Like most Mid-East writings, the Qur'an makes use of allegory. The Qur'an clearly says (Surah III verse 7):

> He it is Who has revealed the Book to you; some of its verses are decisive, they are the basis of the Book; and others are allegorical...

Muslims look upon all humanity as one family under the universal omnipotence of God. Islam rejects the idea that there is a 'chosen people'. They insist that a direct relationship with God is equally open to all alike.

The primary message seen by Muslims is the one God who is not only Lord of the worlds but also:

> the Holy, the Peaceful, the Faithful, the Guardian over his servants, the Shelterer of the orphan, the Guide of the erring, the Deliverer from every affliction, the Friend of the bereaved, the Consoler of the afflicted, in his hand is good, and he is the generous Lord, the Gracious, the Hearer, the

Near at Hand, the Compassionate, the Merciful, the Very Forgiving, whose love for man is more tender than that of the mother-bird for her young.[6]

It thus tries to express the ultimate parameters we associate with full consciousness.

The Muslim emphasis on one God (rather than the hundreds worshipped at the time of Muhammad) does not prevent them from using many word-pictures (like the above) to describe his attributes. However, other forms of expression, like art, pictures, statues, and associated myths come too close to idolatry in their view to be acceptable. Other cultures (for example, Hindus and Catholics) are more comfortable with these diverse modes of expression as symbols of the greater idea that is less expressable. Different peoples clearly have different means of achieving common objectives.

Empathy, in Muslim culture, takes particular forms. One of the basic Muslim pillars is the emphasis on charity and taking care of the poor and the down trodden. Attempting to embody these sentiments in a system of laws, they require that those in the middle and upper income brackets annually distribute among the poor one fortieth of the value of all they possess.

There is much in common among the Jewish, Christian, and Muslim scriptures. In the Qur'an, Jesus is termed the 'Word' of God and bringer of the Gospel. The Catholic theologian, Hans Kung, a pioneer in dialogue among various religions, makes some telling observations about the Qur'an:

Whoever reads the Bible - at least the Hebrew Bible - and the Qur'an in parallel, will be led to ponder whether the three religions of revelation, of Semitic origin, ...could have the same foundation. Is it not one and the same God who speaks in both? Might it not therefore be purely dogmatic prejudice which recognizes Amos and Hosea, Isaiah and Jeremiah, as prophets but not Muhammad?[7]

Kung is willing to call the Qur'an the Word of God, apparently meaning by that the revelation of God in creation. He also asks Muslims to consider whether the Qur'an might also be affected by the humanity and culture of the person and times of Muhammad, as well as being the Word of God. If so, it would be more open to interpretation (as the Old and the New Testaments are open to interpretation in the light of scriptural research).

The road to fuller consciousness is never smooth. As in many religions, there are today diverse factions within the Muslim communities. The more vocal components are fiercely fundamentalist, utterly convinced of the absolute truth of their view and the falsity of all others. On the other hand, some Muslims point out that Muhammad preached religious tolerance and freedom of conscience. Today, we see the same dichotomy that exists in most religions: (1) a conservative, traditionalist desire to restore or reimplement traditional Islamic laws and (2) a reformist call for reinterpretation and reform.[8] The basic question facing Muslims, in common with most other religious believers, is the relation of tradition to modernity. To what extent do we depend on past formulations, and to what extent do we continue to expand our consciousness, understand in broader views, and respond to new socio-historical conditions?

In all this, one can see contradictory movements of love and strife. We are deluged by reports of war, terrorism, and factional separatism in Muslim lands. However, there also is a deep desire for human rights and a non-exclusive community (Qur'an 5:32):

> Whosoever kills a human being for other than manslaughter or corruption in the earth, it shall be as if he had killed all mankind, and whosoever saves the life of one, it shall be as if he had saved the life of all mankind.

Despite the great tendency to political and religious conflict, there are, in many Muslim communities around the world, a quiet perseverance in cultivating the spirit of compassion. There is the underlying push for the survival and further growth in those principles of empathy, agape love, and kindness which are common with all the other great religions of the world. The gradual birth of consciousness continues painfully, despite the gigantic upheavals in some lands.

6.5 FROM THE FAR EAST

In the same time period (1900 BC to present) when the Mid-East religions were under development, the Far-East experienced a parallel evolution in the Hindu, Confucian and Buddhist schools of thought.

Hindu Scriptures

The Hindus have some of the earliest writings on what makes a whole person. Buhlman tells us: "The oldest collection is that of the Vedas which were composed between 1500 and 1200 B.C. ...The Vedas consist of over a thousand psalmlike hymns composed not by authors but 'contemplated' by singers. Later books include the Vedanta which deals with human nature, immortality, blessedness, mysticism and suffering. The Upanishads are concerned mostly with wisdom and faith, the Brahma Sutra with logic or the formulation of knowledge, and the Bhagavad Gita (the Song of the Lord) with discipline and the religious life. In the Bhagavad Gita, God's personal love for people is clearly expressed. ... These books are considered holy writings, the word of God to human beings. They are read, sung, and listened to with reverence. The collections are not closed. Recent texts, such as those of the philosopher S. Radhakrishnan, are considered part of the Vedanta."[9]

Hinduism, as a collection of principles and religious practices, seems to have followed many streams of thought. Historically, Judaism and its offsprings, Christianity and Islam, have carefully separated themselves from all others, stressing differences, while Hinduism has tended to take everything in, accept and absorb all others, finding unity under apparent differences.

Samkya philosophy may contain the oldest theory of evolution, its ideas first starting to take shape about the seventh century B.C., or earlier.[10] Bruteau concludes:

> The whole notion of a temporally immense evolution in which both material and conscious elements are active, which proceeds towards greater complexity and greater consciousness (a higher spiritual life), and which is guided by and drawn to a Divinity beyond the evolution itself, is a fundamental part of the Hindu tradition. Samkya first introduced the view, as a pure philosophy based on reasoning alone, but in the synthesizing atmosphere of the Indian mind it was adopted by all schools of religious thought as well, and even incorporated into scripture (the Bhagavad Gita). It is therefore a mainstream theme in the Hindu consciousness.[11]

In Hinduism there is a basic expectation of a progression of spirit from generation to generation. The idea of a personal reincarnation is one mechanism for this process. It involves a direct effect on a later life by the degree of goodness practiced today.

Another development is the idea of renunciation, moving away from selfishness, and growing towards empathy for others. The Mundaka says:

> But wise, self-controlled, and tranquil souls, who are contented in spirit, and who practice austerity and meditation in solitude and silence are freed from all impurity, and attain by the path of liberation to the immortal, the truly existing, the changeless Self.

> Let him give no thought to transient things, but absorbed in meditation, let him renounce the world.[12]

Some of this philosophy, of course can also be found in the monastics of the Near East and West. However, more recent views in both the East and the West emphasize the goodness of God's entire creation, and our call to be in the world and to help create the 'kingdom of God' in the world. Today, detachment from worldly desires, frustrations, boredom, and pain are usually put in positive terms. The interests of the self must be expanded to include the interests of others, - indeed of the world, even approximating a God's eye view of the human scene. A man's being is gauged by the size of his spirit, that is, the range of reality with which he identifies himself.[13] For example, the person who identifies with his family, finding his joys in theirs, would have that much reality; one who could really identify with mankind as a whole would be of proportionately greater spirit.

There are other common grounds with later developments in the Near East religions. The Mundaka, for example, tells us that the Spirit of God is to be found within each of us:

> Brahman is supreme; he is self-luminous, he is beyond all thought. Subtler than the subtlest is he, farther than the farthest, nearer than the nearest. He resides in the lotus of the heart of every being.[14]

Making conscious contact with that infinite inner resource is the Hindu objective. Our unity with that source hopefully can lead to increasing awareness, and increasing joy. Dasgupta says further, of that unity:

> The Gita not only asserts that all is God, but it also again and again repeats that God transcends all and is simultaneously transcendent and immanent in the world. The answer apparently implied in the Gita to all objections to the apparently different views of the nature of God is that transcendentism, immanentism, and pantheism lose their distinctive and opposite characters in the melting whole of the super-personality of God.[15]

The later influences of the teaching of the New Testament, on the centrality of love, can also be discerned in Hinduism.. Rice, for example, says of Bhakti Yoga, a strong current in the great river of Hinduism:

> ...leading man to God not through knowledge, as in the Vedic past, but through love, piety, intimate communion with and surrender to a Divine Person, the Lord alone. The Lord is conceived as a personal, all powerful, all merciful Being, both transcendent and immanent. He is Love and Infinite Beauty.[16]

Many Hindus acknowledge Christ as a Godman, while believing that there have been others as well, such as Rama, Krishna, and Buddha.

Confucian Thought

Meanwhile, other significant developments were occurring in the great land of China. Born around 550 B.C., Confucius found the Chinese civilization wracked by barbaric feudal warfare and threatened by a disintegration of all social cohesion. Digging into the past writings and traditions, he was determined to deliberately reconstruct what had been the best of Chinese culture. In that editing process, however, he put his own stamp on the result. The tradition he so deliberately established has two particularly relevant components: - Jen and Chun-tzu.

> Jen involves simultaneously a feeling of humanity toward others and respect for oneself, an indivisible sense of the

dignity of human life wherever it appears....the man of Jen is untiringly diligent,... courteous, unselfish, and gifted with empathy.

Having come to the point where he is at home in the universe at large, the Chun-tzu carries the qualities of the ideal host with him through life generally. His approach to others is in terms not of what he can get but of what he can do to accommodate....Poised, confident, and competent,... holding always to his own standards, however others may forget theirs, he is never at a loss as to how to behave and can keep a gracious initiative where others are at sea. Schooled to meet any contingency, 'without fret or fear', his head is not turned by success nor his temper soured by adversity.[17]

Thus, Confucius, too, emphasized that we must realize our inherent dignity and personal worth, that we must use the best that is in us, and that we can strive toward the fulfillment of our great inner potential. Many of the facets of what we call growth of consciousness are in the Confucian teachings, also.

Buddhist Thought

Like many other religions, Hinduism took a turn to excess.[18] Authority became a mechanism for protecting the plush privilege of the Brahmin class. Endless libations, sacrifices, chants, and musicals were available. Tradition was stubbornly preserved till it became a drag on progress. Mystery degenerated into mystification. The injustices of the caste system dehumanized large portions of the population. This turn provided the opportunity for a new movement led by Buddha.

Buddhism came as an outgrowth of Hinduism and spread throughout the orient east of India, which remained Hindu. (True to its traditions, however, Hinduism incorporated many of the Buddhist concepts into a portion of itself. And, when Christianity was introduced into India, some of the knowledge of Jesus and his teachings were likewise incorporated.) Buddha, in the fifth century before Christ, introduced a religion devoid of authority structures, ritual, and tradition. He preached a religion of intense self effort and responsibility. "Those who, relying on themselves only, shall not look for assistance to anyone besides themselves, it is they who shall reach the topmost height."[19]

Buddha's followers spread his teachings, as they remembered them. Realizing that variations were creeping in, many of
the senior priests got together for the purpose of adjusting and
consolidating the words and teaching by mutually reciting what
each thought he had heard, and they spent many a month on their
discussions.[20] The Buddha's teaching itself, the comments added
in later ages, and the Buddhist precepts, all came to be called the
Sanzokyo, or Tripitaka in Sanskrit.

During the time of King Asoka (reigning: 268-232 BC), the
teaching of Buddha Guatama spread throughout the whole of
India and was also being propagated beyond the boundaries of the
country. Missions were sent out to such places as Syria, Egypt,
Kyrene, Macedonia, and Epeiros, spreading Buddhism far and
wide to the western world.[21] In this way, and through the busy
traders of the day, ideas of the East and the Mid-East inter-
mingled.

For the Buddha, the best way of coping with reality was the
complete renunciation of all selfish desires and passions. "The
point of the teaching is to control your own mind. Keep your mind
from greed, and you will keep your behavior right, your mind
pure, and your words faithful. By always thinking about the
transience of your life, you will be able to resist greed and anger,
and will be able to avoid all evils."[22]

The pursuit of 'Emptiness' also became a major part of
Buddhist life. In the western mind, this sometimes is misinterpreted to be an abandonment of life itself. However, there are
some desires that Buddha deliberately advocated; the desire for
the welfare of other beings, for example, and for liberation. In
general, Buddha advocated a 'middle way':

> There are two extremes that should be carefully avoided.
> First, there is the extreme of indulgence in the desires of the
> body. Second, there is the opposite extreme that comes to
> one who wants to renounce this life and to go to an extreme
> of ascetic discipline, torturing one's body and mind
> unreasonably.[23]

The western religions also have a somewhat similar process of
'emptying' oneself of selfishness, hatred, greed, fear, anger, and
so forth. We need to remove nagging feelings of inferiority,
oppressive guilt, and other forms of crippling stress. In both
cultures, these negatives must be set aside to make room in our

consciousness for the positive feelings of empathy, forgiveness, caring love, and kindness. Thus, the process of 'emptying' is important to all.

There is today, however, the complementary concept that the wellsprings of our emotions are basically good and that we can steer them to good purpose. Using that energy in the framework of empathy and caring love gives a positive direction to our actions. Seeking the proper balance between emptying ourselves of controlling desires and using our adult minds to steer the remaining energies is the difficult task we all face.

In Buddhist thought, benevolence and compassion for all suffering beings is of the greatest importance, making Buddhism a religion of love, unity, and tolerance. The basic thread would seem to be a system for living which emphasizes kindness.[24] Buddhists seek to expand one's consciousness so that ultimately boundaries between the person and the surrounding world become blurred. Then, a lasting enlightenment involves a strong sense of unity with all other persons and things. That unity includes empathy for all living creatures. The object of living is not the pursuit of wealth and pleasure, but the increase of virtue and wisdom. The achievement of Buddhahood, then, is perfect wisdom, perfect compassion, perfect power of accomplishing good, and the flowering of the seed of enlightenment which lies within all living beings.

That concept of an Internal Spirit of Goodness, within each person, is common to the religions of the East and the West. In the teachings of Buddha, we find the following:

> Fundamentally, everyone has a pure clean mind, but it is usually covered by the defilement and dust of worldly desires which have arisen from one's circumstances. ... (Persons) must continually remind themselves of this fact by striving to awaken within themselves the pure and unchanging fundamental mind of Enlightenment.

> Buddha-nature exists in everyone no matter how deeply it may be covered over by greed, anger and foolishness, or buried by his own deeds and retribution. Buddha-nature can not be lost or destroyed; and when all defilements are removed, sooner or later it will reappear.[25]

Philosophers over the centuries have wrestled with these concepts and their relation to a universal presence. Though most aspects of

Buddhism avoid the word God, the Buddhist teaching also includes this God-like concept:

> Common people believe that Buddha was born a prince and learned the way to Enlightenment as a mendicant; actually, Buddha has always existed in the world which is without beginning or end. ... Buddha's body is enlightenment itself. Being formless and without substance, it always has been and always will be. It is not a physical body that must be nourished by food. It is an eternal body whose substance is Wisdom.[26]

Buddhism also contains an interesting Buddha trinity:

> Buddha has a three-fold body. (1) Dharma-kaya is the substance of the Dharma, that is, it is the substance of Truth itself...(2) Sambhoga-kaya ...Compassion is the essence of this body, and in its spirit Buddha uses all devices to emancipate all those who are ready for emancipation....(3) Nirmana-kaya signifies that ...Buddha appeared in the world in bodily form and showed the people ...the aspects of the birth, renunciation of this world, and attainment of Enlightenment.[27]

Obviously, the words 'three-fold body' here are used to convey a three-fold phenomena, three expressions of a single reality, rather than merely three separate physical bodies. A similarity to the Christian concept of Father, Holy Spirit, and Son can be discerned.

In much of the teachings of Buddha, one can find a fundamental harmony with the teachings of the Christian gospel. As Fr. J. Kaserow, a Maryknoll Missioner, writes from India: "To be admired in Buddhism (and also in Confucianism and Taoism) are the search for the true self, community as a holy rite, the path to renewal of self, the striving for virtue, the quest for harmony, compassion, the reverence for life and nature, the desire for peace".[28]

This strong reverence for life and nature that is so evident in the Buddhist culture is also found thriving in the Christian traditions, when one looks for it. Consider the parallel of the following Christian writers:

I know well that heaven and earth and all creation are great, generous, and beautiful and good...God's goodness fills all his creatures and all his blessed works full, and endlessly overflows in them...God is everything which is good, as I see it, and the goodness which everything has is God. - Julian of Norwich[29]

...by virtue of the Creation, and still more, of the incarnation, *nothing* here below is profane for those who know how to see. - Teilhard de Chardin[30]

Buddhism thus has many common threads with Western thought. The scriptures of the East and the West are filled with common wisdom if we have the energy and wit to dig it out. Whether we call it achieving Buddha-nature, or seeking Enlightenment, or growing in consciousness, we find in all these scriptures a common purpose for people's lives.

6.6 USING OUR INHERITANCE

Using these tremendous reservoirs of intellectual effort to help us build ourselves and our communities is not usually straightforward. We often get all tangled up in issues and confusions concerning whether writings are truly inspired, what that really means, what interpretation is valid, whether we're victims of a legalistic mentality, and how to integrate the ideas into our lives. Struggling with such issues, however, is also an occasion for personal growth. Rote acceptance and dogmatic presumption do not use the God-given human capability of discernment. The challenge is to build consciousness in the real world of uncertainty and conflict. Without presuming to be authoritative in such matters, we offer the following perspectives for discussion.

Inspiration

Can we accept every word of every scripture as divinely inspired? What does that word 'inspired' mean in practice? The thinking person needs to be careful and perceptive in this, as it affects the way in which the human capability of discernment is employed.

All honest searchers for truth are, we think, invited by their inner spirit to move towards greater harmony with the reality of God's plan. Our hope is that the 'Spirit of God' acts as the spark within each of us, and particularly within the various authors of scriptures. We think it's safe to assume that all of these authors, of Hindu, Buddhist, Jewish, Christian, and Muslim scriptures, were, in some sense, inspired individuals, and were dedicated to their search for truth, with a heartfelt desire to share what they believed were significant contributions. Does that give assurance that these authors are completely and correctly responding to that inspiration?

Most of these religious sayings have passed many critical reviews, by many members of different communities, in successive generations, before being fully accepted. We can reasonably hope that the selection process itself has been guided by that same inner Spirit of God, that urges us towards goodness. So, it's widely believed that many of the outstanding writers, finally selected by the various religious groups for inclusion in their 'canon', were, in fact, inspired by God in an effective way.

We're accustomed to that belief regarding the Jewish and Christian scriptures. We think it is probably also true of much of the Hindu, Buddhist, Muslim, and other scriptures as well, at least in the sense that what was inspired was a message which was important for the progress of peoples at that time and place. It also seems evident that what finally is recorded probably also reflects the humanity of the writer, his or her limitations, and effects of his or her environment.

Interpretation

Tony de Mello, S.J., is reported to have observed that the sacred texts point to God without capturing God's mystery.[31] Scripture, he taught, is like a finger pointing to the moon, so that a person noticing only the finger misses the beauty of the moon. That implies that there's something more to this than a fixed literal interpretation.

Is it possible to have diverse legitimate interpretations of the same text? While that at first seems to take away some of the authority of the text, could it not make the text more valuable in diverse new situations? That would seem to depend on whether the essential message of the original text is preserved, though seen in a different light.

During the past fifty years a tremendous amount of critical

research has been done on the Jewish and Christian scriptures. Many scholars now hold the opinion that the scriptures do contain important historical episodes, but for the most part are rather a proclamation of the faith and philosophy of the writers. The difference is important, for the essential message being transmitted is not dependent on precise historical reporting as in a history textbook. A person can be following a true inspiration, describing a principle of living, and still be imprecise about dates, or use illustrations out of time sequence.

A classic example of this difference, between the message and the carrier of the message, is in Genesis. The writer conveys the message that all of creation is the work of one God, and all that He creates is good. The carrier of the message is the sequence of events in the creation story. This sequence follows closely the creation sequence found in the tablets of the earlier Babylonian civilization.[32] The message, we think, is clearly not a lesson in science. Rather, it teaches the grand power and goodness of God, and the fact that all that we see in the universe is the gift of this one God. The sequence of creation, as the carrier, is consistent with the meager scientific knowledge of that time. We suggest that the sequence of events in the story is the carrier of this message of God's goodness, and nothing more. That view makes irrelevant all the heated arguments of whether these Genesis stories support the theory of evolution or not.

Myth also plays an important role in many early teachings. Misused, the myth can block full understanding. Joseph Campbell, who has devoted his life to the study of myth and symbol, says:

> Historical events are given spiritual meaning by being interpreted mythologically...When you translate the Bible with excessive literalism, you demythologize it. The possibility of a convincing reference to the individual's own spiritual experience is lost...

> The misunderstanding consists in the reading of the spiritual mythological symbols as though they were primarily references to historical events. Localized provincial readings separate the various religious communities. Remythologization - recapturing the mythological meaning - reveals a common spirituality of mankind.[33]

Similarly, the intended message must sometimes be discerned within the language dictated by the times and the circumstances. Knitter, for example, holds that in talking about Jesus, some of the New Testament writers use language not of analytic philosophers (which they were not) but of enthusiastic believers, not of scientists but of lovers.[34] This may color their language without detracting from the core message they wished to convey, which can still be discerned.

Thus, the great gems of truth within writings often have to be extracted from the context in which they were expressed. The modern quest for truth is summarized neatly by Leonard Swidler as probably coming through four processes:

> 1. Historicizing of truth. ... all statements about the truth of the meaning of something are at least partially the product of their historical circumstances.

> 2. The sociology of knowledge. A statement about the true meaning of things will be partially determined by the speaker's geographic, cultural, class, etc., perspective.

> 3. The limitations of language. Truth as the meaning of something is deabsolutized by the limits of human language, which can express things from only one perspective at once.

> 4. Hermeneutics. ...All knowledge is interpreted knowledge; anything can be studied only through the categories we provide, within the horizon we establish, under the paradigm we utilize, and in response to the questions we raise.[35]

Despite all these difficulties, the results of studying the Scriptures can be truly remarkable. The input into them is made up of words from a human mouth or a hand, guided, at least in part, by the divine. As a light illumines a room, God's word was a light for the particular time in which it was spoken. The amazing thing about God's word is that it can be transported to a different time and place, and illumine a different scene with great clarity.

Each person has special needs, according to their situation in life. What is sought from Bible reading therefore varies with each person. Have we not observed that God-directed persons, in their attempt to get further positive direction from the holy writings, do get new insights that vary according to their individual needs? The benefit, however, seems to be in proportion to the effort of the reader to become oriented to God's love. It's somewhat like the full enjoyment of a beautiful song when the singer puts her whole person into the song-writer's original spirit.

It seems that those who strive to love God and their fellow man become better people through reading inspired words, as the flow of God's spirit is not hampered by their spirits. For these readers, biblical interpretations seem always to reinforce kind and empathetic behavior, whether they be interpretations of historical books, of parables, of apocalyptic literature, or of myth. Thus, one loving person initiating the flow of God's spirit can affect another in a positive manner, even though centuries come between the initiator and the receiver. Surprisingly, the living God can change us today, through our reading the long past life of Abraham.

A further startling possibility is that two God-enraptured people can come up with two different interpretations, and these seemingly opposing interpretations will both aid these two different people into a more loving direction, each for his own life. The prophet spoke God's inspired word of love; and from that word, God's spirit flows across the centuries through each of us. With that connection, the present day reader may be helped to become a prophet in his own time.

Therefore, recognizing both the inspiration of the writers, their own limitations, and the importance of our own disposition, we have some work to do in extracting the meanings from scriptures, that are applicable to our world today. We need to look to our trusted communities to see what consensus we find in our common searches for meaning in the scriptures. Together, we can avoid some of the more obvious misinterpretations of which we are capable. Finding appropriate meanings must benefit from the best critical research of which our scholars are capable (and which we have the time to absorb). Most important, however, our search must be done with an open mind, always ready for a better insight. Each of us must search for the improved interpretation that illuminates the benevolent plan of God for us.

The wisdom of thousands of years of human experience is there; the rewards are well worth the work needed to extract that portion of the wisdom which is applicable today to each one of us, individually.

Legalism

There is another very significant issue common to the use of all sacred scriptures, and that is the issue of legalism. In every culture, the scriptures have been followed by the promulgation of laws and regulations which supposed authorities believe are the practical embodiment of the teachings in the scriptures. These laws and regulations attain a life of their own.

What's wrong with legalism, anyway? Laws and regulations are usually meant for the good of the individual or the common good. They're the voice of experience, like signposts that warn of dangerous shoals or sharp curves in the road. What frequently happens in established societies, however, is that the laws and regulations multiply, applying to more and more specific situations, and even to situations which are not yet very clear. Then, increasing emphasis must be placed on adherence to them all, to maintain respect for the law. Soon, the adherence becomes the major focus of effort; people begin, unconsciously, to believe that these laws and regulations are the primary if not the total objective. They put in second place, and tend to forget, the more fundamental needs to creatively exercise mercy, forgiveness, justice, compassion, empathy, caring love, and kindness. The law itself becomes for them a God; and a form of idolatry ensues, practiced in a mechanical, impersonal, and dehumanizing way.

Legalism also makes it difficult to recognize that some laws and regulations are needed for some times and places and not for others. Individual conscience is replaced by blind conformity. Newer insights are more difficult to accept. Guilt builds up needlessly around regulations whose value may have ceased long ago.

Jesus preached, on the other hand, the fulfillment of the original purposes of the law, without the distracting excesses of legalism. He preached a return to the free exercise of loving God and loving neighbor, as fully conscious persons. Jesus protested against the legalism of the Scribes and the Pharisees of his time. As Hans Kung observes: "The focal concern of Jesus, himself, was to overcome legalism by the fulfillment of the Word of God in love, in view of the coming Reign."[36]

Over the centuries, however, and even today, one finds supposed Christians, as well as members of all other faiths, succumbing to the distraction of excessive legalism. We continue to need a stronger emphasis on Jesus' replacement of legalism with the more basic empathy, love, and forgiveness. Then one might see more laws and regulations first judged by their legislators for their contribution to those three effects. If that occurred, one would expect that people would feel more liberated, not from the law but from the legalism. A deeper understanding could also be gained of a God who loves and suffers with people, rather than one who rules them under law.

Writing the books of scripture was meant to be an act of great empathy, by most writers, to set down the inspiration of God, for the rest of humanity. Out of love for us, the writers labored to set down what they believed to be of the utmost importance for our well being, both now and hereafter. Readers of the scriptures invariably obtain helpful illuminations of the ways in which present day situations can be handled. Each persistent reader, it seems, receives a spark of inspiration, even though the reading itself is only peripherally relevant to the current need. So, despite the difficulties of discerning the original intent, despite the complications of ancient cultures, and despite the attempts by some to over-legalize the interpretations, the scriptures remain a great asset. They remain valuable aids to everyone's finding the paths to personal fulfillment.

Personal integration

These ancient writings become a part of the heritage of later generations, and thus become re-interpreted in the light of the consciousness and needs of the day. We each attempt to interpret what we read in the context of our accumulated convictions. We attempt to integrate this into a broader consciousness. That process of interpretation and integration must be a very personal endeavor. It relates to the formation of one's own ideals and identity. A small part of that process, in which we each set a future direction for ourselves, might be illustrated in a personal interpretation of the Ten Commandments, as follows:

1. YOU SHALL HONOR NO OTHER GOD BUT ME.

   Against: idolatry of self, others, things like: money, sex, power, or the state.

   For: seeking with an open mind an ultimate understanding of the mind of God; pursuing the way of living that our inner conscience teaches us and our believing community reinforces.

2. YOU SHALL NOT MISUSE THE NAME OF GOD.

Against: the use of God-given authority for unworthy, self-serving purposes; disrespect for: the concept of God, his creation, the principles he stands for, or the spark of God in every person.

For: the use of God-given authority in a manner that grants freedom and builds dignity in those governed; respect for: the mystery of God, the beauty of all creation, the dignity of all persons as children of God, and their potential value in the sight of God regardless of their imperfections.

3. YOU SHALL KEEP HOLY THE SABBATH

Against: ignoring the reality of God and our role in his plan for humankind; refusal to acknowledge God's love and forgiveness; separating our daily lives from consciousness of God's creative action.

For: ever increasing gratitude and joy for God's gift of life and the opportunity to grow; taking time for renewing our awareness of God, deepening our relation to God, and re-committing to the way of living taught by God; reflecting on belief in a loving and forgiving God who seeks to dwell in every person and wills the free growth and fulfillment of every person; freeing ourselves from fear and guilt in the light of that love.

4. YOU SHALL HONOR YOUR FATHER AND MOTHER

Against: any force or influence that weakens family life or community solidarity.

For: that behavior which builds loving relationships, within the family and in diverse communities beyond the family.

5. YOU SHALL NOT KILL

Against: physical or mental violence to others; denying the sacredness of human life, denying others their dignity, or dehumanizing others.

For: the honoring of every human life, with respect, empathy, caring love, and kindness; and the creation of environments which permit freedom, justice, and the full growth of every human being.

6. YOU SHALL NOT COMMIT ADULTERY

Against: treating persons solely as sex objects, and dehumanizing sexuality.

For: human dignity and fulfillment of the total person, - mind, heart and body, - spiritual and physical, in covenant love and in harmony with our Creator.

7. YOU SHALL NOT STEAL

Against: stealing personal property, economic exploitation of any kind, denying essential human rights, discrimination, separatism, reducing personal respect and dignity; and withholding forgiveness.

For: justice for all, caring for the poor and underprivileged, overcoming institutional injustice or oppression, and granting forgiveness generously.

8. YOU SHALL NOT BEAR FALSE WITNESS AGAINST YOUR NEIGHBOR.

Against: lying, cheating, ruining another's reputation, deceit for personal gain, and demeaning others.

For: truthfulness, speaking always with kindness, speaking to build rather than destroy another's self worth; listening, out of respect for the worth of every person.

9. YOU SHALL NOT COVET YOUR NEIGHBOR'S WIFE.

Against: Unbridled lust, and permission of disordered passions.

For: the conscious steering of all human emotion; recognizing the value of all humans as wonderful creations of God and worthy of caring love and reverence; and emptying ourselves of narrow selfishness.

10. YOU SHALL NOT COVET YOUR NEIGHBOR'S GOODS.

Against: greed, exploiting others, and despoiling the environment.

For: valuing personal relationships above material goods; creating and using wealth for constructive purposes; love of creation, and loving care for the world's environment.

Thus, we can use scripture promptings to help us to reflect on present day knowledge and needs, and to set our future course. This can greatly augment the meaning and value of scriptures. We feel that this is not in any way a rejection of past writers. It is rather the full use of these tools for the better understanding of our place, our purpose, and our promise. It is the God-intended process of discernment and growth in perception, for which God has endowed us and destined us. It incorporates the writings of the past into the current, on-going process of growth in consciousness.

6.7 EMPHASIS ON CONSCIOUSNESS

As seen in the above reviews of the scriptures, there is a clear thread of emphasis on consciousness, including empathy, caring-love, and kindness, in all of the major religions. A practical example of that commonality is indicated by the presence of the 'golden rule' in all of their scriptures. Witness the following:[37]

Islam: "No one of you is a believer until he desires for his brother that which he desires for himself." (Sunnah)

Christianity: "So always treat others as you would like them to treat you; that is the meaning of the Law and the Prophets." (Matthew 7:12)

Judaism: "What is hateful to you, do not to your fellowman. That is the entire Law; all the rest is commentary." (Talmud, Shabbat 31a)

Zoroastrianism: "That nature alone is good which refrains from doing unto another whatsoever is not good for itself." (Dadistan-i-dinik, 94,5)

Taoism: "Regard your neighbor's gain as your own gain, and your neighbor's loss as your own loss." (T'ai Shang Kan Ying P'ien)

Confucianism: "Is there one maxim which ought to be acted upon throughout one's whole life? Surely it is the maxim of loving kindness: Do not unto others what you would not have them do unto you." (Analects 15,23)

Buddhism: "Hurt not others in ways that you yourself would find hurtful." (Udana-Varga 5,18)

Brahmanism: "This is the sum of duty: Do naught unto others which would cause you pain if done to you." (Mahabharata, 5,1517)

These wise admonitions are indeed hard to follow when the other persons are apparently so different or have come from a very different culture or upbringing. Nevertheless, the near universal golden rule challenges us to imaginatively create a greater social understanding of the other's condition, putting ourselves in the other's place, and giving of ourselves. The practicality of this, in large and very small things, is emphasized in the Buddhist definition of five kinds of offerings:

1) offering kind words to others.
2) offering a soft countenance with a smile,
3) offering a warm glance to others,
4) offering a compassionate heart to others, and
5) the physical offering (of one's labor or even one's life)[38]

We see this thread of consciousness as a basic tenet of all the major religious streams in the world. Moreover, we see a gradually growing emphasis on the centrality of consciousness, despite many other distractions. Men and women become distinctly different in this mode of living. There develops a 'loving spirit', and a 'fighting-spirit', which gives us determination to act in full consciousness. There is the sort of 'team spirit' whereby we know we're part of a greater cause. That growth brings about a unity of the human spirit with that of the Divine Providence. These are the common factors which promote the evolution of consciousness. Their gradual acceptance, we suggest, constitutes the painful birth of the true spirit of humankind, in accord with the urgings of that inner light, which we call the Holy Spirit.

6.8 PERSONAL FULFILLMENT IN THE COMMON MINISTRY

It seems very probable that we are all perceiving a single reality but from different perspectives. It's our hope and belief that it is the same spirit that works lovingly in all men and women of good will, in every culture. As long as we remain in this spirit, we can be in cooperating community with all those who dwell throughout the earth, who are similarly in-spirit. All of these streams of religious thought contribute to the global enhancement of the highest levels of consciousness, of which humankind is capable. They thus each contribute to the continuous birthing of the Spirit of God in the hearts of people everywhere, from age to age. We can be universally grateful for this.

It's when we give priority to the selfish aspects of our humanity, that the trouble starts. We sometimes tend to think that the way we saw it is the exact and only way it can be seen. We start arguing about the details. We perhaps find that it gives us power to be the 'ones who know', that is, - the only chosen ones, the stars of the show on Mount Olympus or other. The desire for uniqueness and power can lure us off the right track.

It's interesting to contemplate how Jesus, Buddha, Confucius, and many other great leaders did not seek power. Rather, they lived the teachings of compassion and forgiveness. But those who focus instead on seeking power will often get only power. It's painfully apparent that when some are set too much on ruling other persons, through power, they lose the capacity to inspire others or to lead others to greater consciousness. The emphasis subtly shifts to other things, even though the words are little changed. If this happens, then the fundamental movement towards inter-related consciousness, and hence personal fulfillment, is inhibited and may be thwarted.

Despite these many imperfections, one can observe many islands of truly loving communities, and a common thread of personal fulfillment through genuine ministry, in all of the above religions. What matters primarily, and what really works, is ministry or service to other people. What's needed are more people who are willing to give of their body and blood - that is, all that they are, in the service of humanity. Through this they more readily become united with their fellow human beings and so also united with their provident God. This can be and is largely inclusive of all faiths.

Consider, for example, Mother Theresa of Calcutta. She has Christians, Buddhists, Hindus, and persons of any type of faith working with her in the necessity of helping the poor, who likewise are of all faiths. There are, in fact, endless opportunities for such common ministries. There are groups who work in shelters for the homeless, in prison ministries, and in hospitals, which include persons of many faiths, working for persons of all faiths. Such 'service to others' groups pledge and dedicate themselves to the service of God and man. That these groups may be sponsored by one or another faith is a compliment to that faith, and is not a serious impediment to the common ministry. In fact, the services of an institutional church often stimulate broader expressions of love and solidarity. That leadership encourages others, of the same or different faiths, to join lovingly in such enterprises.

The sense of satisfaction is great for these people who put their whole beings on the line. This is not a safe and secure life in the usual sense. The paradox is that despite the apparent losses, through a neglect of things which conventional wisdom says are important, their lives and their spirits are evidently enriched. They acquire a sense of spiritual union with other persons and with their God; their lives are often joyful and relatively free of anxiety; and they acquire a real conviction of their personal value.

This, then, is the key to the notion of unity. It is not unity through conformity. It is not an attempt to make us all alike in our viewpoints of reality. Rather, it is simply unity through caring love. That unity becomes more evident as each religion further emphasizes its basic concepts of empathy, caring love, kindness, and service for all persons everywhere. The bonds of consciousness among all persons of good will can be tremendously strong. Those bonds can exist despite our differences, and even can be stronger because of them. We can rejoice in the beauty of our

Figure 6: Emanating with Empathy, Caring Love,
and Kindness, Are Gifts Like Forgiveness,
Fortitude, Patience, Creativity, and Joy

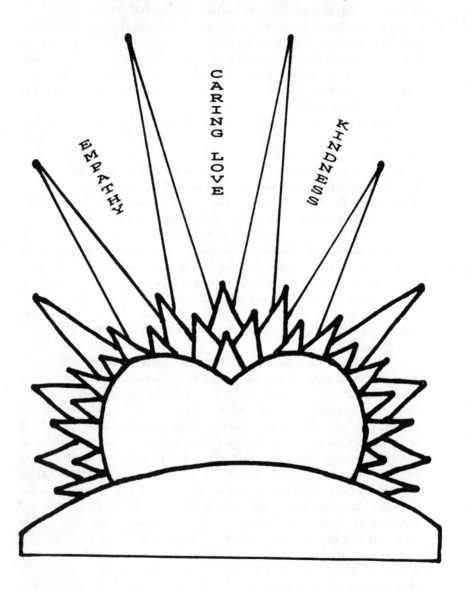

diversity. This potential unity is a lesson from all of creation and a lesson from history.

This growth of consciousness around the world, through service to others, is contributed to by people of many faiths, having a common direction. Among these religions there exists a priceless heritage of thought gleaned from thousands of years of honest searching by gifted and inspired men and women. Still, the burden for progress now lies primarily on the mass of persons who must freely build their individual consciousness. In the final analysis, it is all of us together who determine the rate of growth of world consciousness and thus the pace of the birth of the Spirit of God on earth.

REFERENCES

[1]P. Carus, *The History of the Devil, and Idea of Evil*, Land's End Press, N.Y., N.Y., 1969, pp. 29–40.

[2]R.E. Murphy, *Wisdom Literature*, Grand Rapids, Mi., 1981, p. 11.

[3]*Webster's Collegiate Dictionary*, Merriam Co., Springfield, MA, 1947.

[4]Rabbi William B. Silverman, *The Jewish Concept of Man*, B'nai B'rith Youth Organization, Washington, D.C., 1976. pp. 11–14.

[5]Huston Smith, *The Religions of Man*, Harper and Row, New York, 1958, p. 339.

[6]Ameer Ali, *The Spirit of Islam*, Christophers, London, 1923, p. 150.

[7]H. Kung, "Interreligious and Interideological Dialogue: The Matrix for All Systematic Reflection Today," presented at the conference Toward a Universal Theology of Religion, Temple University, Oct 17–19, 1984, reported in *J. Ecumenical Studies*, vol. 22 no. 1, winter, 1985, p. 197.

[8]John L. Esposito, "Islam Today: Back to the Future", *National Catholic Reporter*, November 28, 1986, pp. 11–15.

[9]W. Buhlmann, *God's Chosen Peoples*, Orbis Books, Marynoll, N.Y.

[10]Troy Wilson Organ, *The Hindu Quest For The Perfection of Man*, Ohio University, Athens, 1970, p. 305.

[11]Beatrice Bruteau, *Evolution Toward Divinity*, The Theosophical Publishing House, Wheaton, Ill., 1974, p. 121.

[12]Swami Prabhavananda and Frederick Manchester, *The Upanishads*, American Library, N.Y., 1957, p. 44.

[13]Huston Smith, *loc. cit.*, pp. 30–31.

[14]Swami Prabhavananda and Frederick Manchester, *loc. cit.*, p. 47.

[15]Surentranath Dasgupta *A History of Indian Philosophy*, The University Press, Cambridge, 1922-55, Vol. II, p. 527.

[16]Edward Rice, *The Five Great Religions*, Bantam Books, N.Y., 1973, p. 35.

[17]Huston Smith, *The Religions of Man*, Harper and Row, New York, 1958, pp. 179-180.

[18]Huston Smith, *loc. cit.*, pp. 101-104.

[19]E.A.Burtt, ed., *The Teachings of the Compassionate Buddha*, Mentor Books, New York, 1955, p. 50.

[20]Bukkyo Dendo Kyokai, *The Teaching of Buddha*, Kosaido Printing Co., Ltd., Tokyo, Japan, 1985, pp. 282-283.

[21]*ibid.*, pp. 272-273.

[22]*ibid.*, p. 11.

[23]*ibid.*, p. 57.

[24]Bukkyo Dende Kyokai, *The Teachings of Buddha*, Sangodo Printing Co., Ltd. Tokyo, seventeenth edition, 1972.

[25]Bukkyo Dendo Kyokai, *The Teaching of Buddha*, Kosaido Printing Co., Ltd., Tokyo, Japan, 1985, pp. 68, 78.

[26]*ibid.*, pp. 22, 26.

[27]Matthew Fox, *Original Blessing*, Bear & Co., Santa Fe, New Mexico, p. 304.

[28]John Kaserow, "Why Jesus", *Maryknoll*, Feb., 1985, pp. 37-40.

[29]Julian of Norwich - cited on p. 43 of Matthew Fox, *Original Blessing*, Bear & Co., Santa Fe, New Mexico.

[30]Teilhard De Chardin, *The Divine Milieu*, Harper Torchbooks, N.Y., N.Y.,1965, p. 66.

[31]Thomas H. Stahel "'Tell Us,' They Asked, 'What is God Like?' - An Appreciation of Tony de Mello, S.J.", *America*, Dec. 12, 1987, pp. 446-450.

[32]A.H. Sayce, *Records of the Past*, New Series, Vol I, pp. 128-131.

[33]Eugene Kennedy, *The Now and Future Church*, Doubleday & Co., Garden City, N.Y., 1985, pp. 83-84.

[34]Paul F. Knitter,*No Other Name?*, Orbis Books, Maryknoll, N.Y.,1985, p. 185.

[35]L. Swidler, "Interreligious and Interideological Dialogue: The Matrix for All Systematic Reflection Today," presented at the conference Toward a Universal Theology of Religion, Temple University, Oct 17-19, 1984, reported in *J. Ecumenical Studies*, vol. 22 no. 1, winter, 1985, p. 194.

[36]H. Kung, *ibid.*, p. 197.

[37]Lewis Browne, *The World's Great Scriptures*, Macmillan Co., New York, 1946, p. xv.

[38]Bukkyo Dendo Kyokai, *The Teaching of Buddha*, Kosaido Printing Co., Ltd., Tokyo, Japan, 1985, p. 170.

7

POSITIONING TODAY

The growth of wisdom, discussed in the preceding chapter, does not happen in a vacuum. In modern times, the dynamics of interaction, debate, and consensus are aided by communications and broader education among more persons. Still, the essential component is the somewhat isolated search for truth, in which each person engages. That individual search is an inherent part of each person's growth in consciousness.

Individuals are inspired to crystallize their positions out of the best of the milieu they live in. They rely in part on a trust of other individuals and communities. Their own views build upon the views of those they trust, and then they add their own stamp to the product. The individual positions, resulting from many lonely searches, then contribute to the ocean of thought in which people live and breathe.

In this personal search, we eventually come across the need to position ourselves relative to the diverse ideas about the creator of it all. We find we want to add depth and breadth to our vision of life, as we include a relationship to the Divine Providence. We each need to find at least a temporary place to stand. We need to pick at least some parts of the inheritance about God which seem to be firm enough for us to act upon.

Given the ups and downs of so many religious movements, the long road of discernment, and the somewhat amazing and complex inheritance, many have disavowed any position at all. Each person needs to struggle to find his own solid ground. It seems that only with a struggle, to reasonably relate ourselves to a Divine Providence, can we get that inner assurance that our lives can be in harmony with a purpose beyond our trivial pursuits.

7.1 FAITH AND COMMITMENT

Every once in a while, someone asks the unthinkable question: "Over the centuries, could all those writers of scripture, discussed in chapter 6, have been misled?" Realizing that there must be a considerable uncertainty about most things, and especially about a reality beyond our senses, they ask, "How can one have any faith in a Divine Providence, today? What is faith, anyway? And similarly, regarding the future, how can one reasonably hope?" Every thinker, down through the ages, must have asked the same questions. What should be our process of discernment? Surely, it would be imprudent, and certainly a betrayal of humankind's capacity for reflection, to blindly accept every attractive speculation. Even the most authoritative offerings have had need of critical examination prior to acceptance, as a study of history would indicate. That does seem to leave us somewhat on our own, and in dangerous seas. How can one proceed?

As human beings, we are blessed with some good tools to help us. We each have the ability to reflect, and to examine the consistency of one fact in relation to all the others on which we place some reliance. For a given hypothesis, we search for inconsistencies and we discard portions that are too dubious or unnecessary. We modify those portions, or reinterpret those portions that do not fit well enough to our basic beliefs. In some cases, we will consider altering basic beliefs, to accommodate a new hypothesis, but that is done only cautiously. Often we can defer acceptance of some portions of the hypothesis, in favor of focusing on more essential parts.

Beyond this, our examination clearly must include adequate consideration of views from others whom we respect. A careful balancing of our own judgements against those of others must be made, with an inherent assignment of probable quality to each. In this balancing, we must be open to the wisdom of others; but we will naturally be more receptive to those that we already trust and respect. Even with them, however, the preservation of personal integrity requires that every key input be subject to the same test of 'fit' with our very basic and very personal beliefs.

At some point, we may experience a sense of illumination, when a hypothesis (or a portion thereof) seems to be plausible. Finally, it 'fits well'; it is, as far as we can tell, consistent with a wide range of other knowledge we depend upon greatly. At this point, one is finally in a position to make a great leap from the intellectual satisfaction of plausibility to the decision for a commitment. A rational faith always involves such a carefully considered decision. It is a decision to make a commitment to a hypothesis that finally appears to be utterly plausible. With that commitment may go the building of love, loyalty, and trust in the object of our commitment. With that commitment also goes the resolve to make the hypothesis a basis for action in our lives. That resolve can be very strong, indeed, despite the fact that the whole process starts with a recognized uncertainty.

The growing or weakening of our commitment then depends on the subsequent reinforcements or convincing counter-arguments that we receive. These come first from our own repeated reexaminations and recommitments, and second from the convictions of other trusted members of our community. This faith, then, is not a once and for all event, but a continuing development, with a constant state of tension between present position and alternatives. It is not certainty or perfection, but a well-considered, strong adherence to hypotheses, along with periodic testing of those hypotheses.

This faith does not, obviously, insure that the hypothesis is reality. The above type of faith can, nevertheless, achieve a total personal commitment, through the full exercise of our capacity and responsibilities as a person. It equips us to use a hypothesis with conviction. It then enables us to periodically reexamine the hypothesis in the light of our own circumstances and experience. If necessary, we can seek a reinterpretation of the hypothesis in that new light. In effect, doubt and questioning are an essential part of the process of further discernment. Any reinterpretation, then, is not considered to be a loss of faith or hope, but a continuation of the process of acquiring the same. Such faith, we believe, retains and builds our identity and our fulfillment as persons, able to use our God-given gifts of intellect.

Thus faith can be very far from simply and blindly accepting a body of knowledge that someone else has handed to you. It has no relation to the fabled opium (as per Marx) that some accept at any price so as to ease their fears or sense of insecurity. That attitude may in fact bind one to an immobile and static existence. It is real faith only when one has descended into the pits, as it were, and has found that there are no absolute facts to stand on, and has accepted that an element of uncertainty must remain. It is faith only when one then has wrestled with basic hypotheses, found them to be plausible, and finally resolved to base one's life on those hypotheses, despite that element of uncertainty.

Faith must, therefore, be a very personal thing. Belief can only come out of the depths of one's heart and experience. But after all the searching, it finally is like getting out of the safe boat and walking to God on the water.

Hope is an inseparable companion of faith. Discouragement, depression, and even despair are common pitfalls, given the frequent problems that beset every person. The future progress of our kind, and even the existence of a guiding spirit to a better state, are uncertain. Yet, we have a marvelous capacity to draw deeply from some inner strength and to generate hope in even the worst circumstances. The gem of hope overcomes and even thrives on uncertainty. In a sense, we are greater with uncertainty than we could be without it. Some would even say that the full development of the person only comes after one has passed through a period of disbelief and near-despair, and then builds a base of hope. Saints have their 'dark night of the soul'.

In the struggle for discernment, we need not be alone. In order to be true persons, with a unique individuality, we each must and will see things differently and interpret things differently. Each view is necessarily limited in scope and understanding. Recognizing the limitations of each person's viewpoint, it is prudent and fittingly humble to recognize that there is no one-person's viewpoint that is right in all respects. Just as a second eye gives us new perspective in a third dimension, so too do different viewpoints often illuminate an obscure truth. Moreover, our faith is not a static, once and for all decision, but a growing, changing thing, - a process that gradually draws us to closer harmony with God's process.

Therefore, we do band together in faith communities when our faiths are similar. By this we give to each other moral support and help one another in sorting out our confusions and arriving at some degree of consensus. Since we accept the hypothesis of a loving Divine Providence that intends our evolving growth in consciousness, we expect some loving assistance from God in this evolution of faith. We live in the hope that, with God's help, the members of the church community, and hence the church itself, will acquire a clearer perception of reality, and so grow in consciousness of both our fellow persons and the Divine Providence. This, we trust, will occur (sometimes most gradually or erratically) despite the obvious weaknesses, failures and errors of individual members of that church community and of its leaders.

Our faith, then, nurtured by a loving community, provides a framework within which we continue to build our personhood and seek personal fulfillment. If well established, our faith becomes a rock that we can hang onto when things get rough. Moreover, it can give us that awareness of a larger universe, within which we may find greater purpose and deeper meaning.

7.2 IMAGES OF GOD

How do we now relate to God? We use approximate models of a far greater reality, which we can barely understand. Do the older and still popular images of God 'fit' with the emphasis on growing consciousness? How do these images 'fit' with reality as we now see it? For each of us, another look may be worthwhile.

Actually, it seems that no human has a very clear idea of God. If we knew all about God, we would be as great as God, and we could take over the job and the job title. Fortunately, that awesome responsibility is beyond our grasp. The old Apophatic tradition (of heroes like Saint John of the Cross, Saint Theresa Avilla, and Meister Eckhart), recognized God as partly unknowable. Yet, we need some tentative characterization of God, as best we can discern it, as a basis for our relationship to God.

Each of us tries to visualize God in his own way. To some extent, we tend to make God into our own image. We each have a set of experiences, in which we encounter gratuitous goodness and a renewal of our hope; and we tend to formulate our image of God consistent with those experiences.[1] Early religion, in speaking of unknown power, was hesitant to call it male or female; but some groups seized on the female and others made their divinity-word male. The Hebrews had a female word 'Shekinah' meaning God's Spirit of wisdom. The Assyrs had a female name of Astarte to describe a powerful goddess. Our culture favors an image of a male God. We have Michaelangelo's grey-haired grandfather on the ceiling of the Sistine Chapel. Actually, most would agree that God is beyond male and female character-istics; the divine mystery must be more than the best traits of both sexes.

Some ancient Jewish people saw God, at least in part, as having the characteristics of a great leader, leading his people out of slavery to a promised land, and guiding them in subsequent battles. The Muslims see God as a unity, although this unity is described by 100 names, that speak of many characteristics unified in one infinite power. The Christians see God as a unity also, but this unity has three separate appearances, or persons, Father, Son, and Holy Spirit. More of this later.

In Hinduism, we are given many representations of God. Different characteristics of God are described by statues rather than by words. God's power is represented by a many-armed statue; his love by a nursing mother. Behind all these representa-tions, the loving Hindu sees a unity, that is beyond these representations, and which cares about his daily needs and his eventual salvation.

The Buddhist speaks of the eternal Buddha which always has been and always will be, an eternal body whose substance is wisdom. For them there is a state of perfect blessedness, achieved by the absorption of the soul into the supreme spirit.

The Pantheist states that everything is God and *God is everything*. Avoiding that extreme, the Panentheist says that *God is in everything* and everything is in God.[2]

Some groups within Protestantism, Islam, and Judaism, emphasize the transcendence of God, beyond the physical uni-verse, 'out there'. Other groups in those same professions, and in Catholicism and certain forms of Hinduism, acknowledge this transcendence, but also emphasize God's immanence or presence within the universe. For example, the Catholic theologian Richard McBrien says:

The Catholic vision sees God in and through all things: other people, communities, movements, events, places, objects, the world at large, the whole cosmos. The visible, the tangible, the finite, the historical - all these are actual or potential carriers of the Divine Presence. Indeed, it is only in and through these material realities that we can encounter the invisible God.[3]

Thus, one finds many complementary images of God. However, all of these images are necessarily incomplete, and limited by our own ignorance and our inability to comprehend so vast a reality. Yet, if we look sympathetically, we find that most images in different cultures convey something positive that helps people to act lovingly, cooperatively and constructively. This, it would seem, is often more important than any pretense at accuracy or any attempts to achieve an ego-inflating uniformity of view. We can be more sympathetic to these different views if we remember that each of these inadequate images are meant to aid the perception of a reality that is far beyond the images themselves. Certainly it is human nature to seek ever better models of the distant unknown; but perfection is not necessary in order for models to be extremely useful.

As we formulate our purpose and direction in this life, each of us needs to find, within our community's consensus, a personal 'place to stand' concerning our relation to divinity. On our part, we, the authors, felt the need to reexamine our ideas about God, the relationships with God that these ideas imply, and how they harmonize with the concept of growing consciousness. What portions of our inheritance do we now particularly favor? What images do we now find comfortable, as reference points in our lives? Each person will refashion his or her ideas somewhat differently, but often there is much in common in the basics.

We find that our basic ideas can be made to fit well with the probable phenomena of humankind's growth in consciousness and with our projection of this growth into the plan of a Divine Providence. In the following, we sketch the journey we, the authors, have taken, in our own searching. We hasten to add that it's only one example of a personal searching, and each reader will find differences between our finding and his or her own perceptions.

7.3 THE SPIRIT WITHIN US

Earlier, we had noted the disconcerting tendencies we have toward local optimization. There are many easy roads to dissipa-

Figure 7: The Many Ways in Which
We Convey the Presence of Divinity

tion. Entropy, the loss of order, often seems to be a natural destiny. Despite our best intentions, we often seem to lose important ground. On the other hand, we also noted the long term drift, over millions of years, to higher consciousness. We hypothesized that this trend is not by chance, but indicates the effect of a loving force for progress, a Divine Providence.

We have the choice of cooperating with this force or not, of aligning ourselves with this evolution or going against it. That force is experienced in a personal way. The possibility of choosing a better decision is repeatedly apparent. Once a person acquires even a partial habit of seeking broader consciousness, it can become relevant in everything the person does. It's as if we were always invited to make positive decisions and take positive actions by some higher level of consciousness, - a spark or spirit within us. We can resolve to accept this invitation and devote ourselves to the perceived positive direction.

But what is this word 'spirit'? One is reminded of the common expressions 'fighting spirit' and 'team spirit' which connote an inner energy that marshals deep resources and gives them a direction. One can have similar springs of motivation and energy to act in fulfillment of a deeply held ideal or quest. So too, one can be strongly moved to realize the goal of greater consciousness, so as to experience greater empathy, caring love, and kindness.

One way of defining this phenomena of internal invitation is to relate it to the larger concept of Divine Providence. That internal invitation, one can hypothesize, is due to the Spirit of God acting in persons and offering an invitation to the ideal. The person can choose to harmonize all actions towards that goal. Some would say that the person then is "filled with the Holy Spirit", meaning that the person deliberately accepts the direction of the Divine Providence as his own, and commits inner resources to that quest. As this awareness of purpose grows, the sense of unity with the divine plan matures. The person repeatedly chooses to align his or her life in harmony with that plan, to achieve the goal of greater consciousness. In effect, the invitation of the Spirit of God is accepted as the guiding direction in that life. The person remains open to that guidance, convinced that the resulting direction will lead to personal fulfillment.

We find reinforcement of these ideas of the Spirit of God acting in us in many more recent authors as well. The growth of complexity and consciousness, in the long evolution of the earth, is theorized by the philosopher - scientist, Teilhard de Chardin. In his view, that evolutionary growth is accompanied by a closer and closer union with the divine. A consistent corollary, it seems, is in the concepts of an immanent God by present day 'process theologians'. Pittenger, for example, also sees a spark of God in all of creation:

> God is ever incarnating himself in his creation, which means that he is ever entering into it - not as if he were absent from it and intervened now and again in it, but in the deeper sense that he ... ever energizes in nature and in history, and above all in the lives of men, expressing himself more and more fully, until the whole created order becomes, in some sense, 'the body of God'. It is *all* incarnation, in fact; but it is not on some uniformitarian level, for there are heights and depths, a more or less, a here and a there, in the process.[4,5]

Troeltsch also describes this 'God within us' idea and argues that the human spirit, or the human being's self-experience, gives imposing testimony of the immanence of God within our very being.[6] Our own self-awareness, our constant searching for more, our innate need to trust, and to love, - all such experiences seem to point to an active presence of an absolute spirit in finite things.

Rahner, too, talks about a "communion with the one true God, and an experience of purpose, peace, and growth for the individual and society." Such an encounter, he says, is experienced in a variety of real-life situations:

> It is contained in the 'fundamental option' by which we choose to live our lives not only for ourselves but for others. It is implied in every act of freedom by which we take on responsibility for others, or trust - in the face of death or meaninglessness, or experience the deep beauty or wrenching demands of commitment to another human being or to a humanitarian cause.[7]

It seems we are offered many gifts, as opportunities to shape our personhood, if only we'll marshal our being to accept the gifts, and strive to become the person envisioned. 'Mister T', the popular TV star, is a black man of giant physical-proportions and determination, with an Apache Indian haircut. His posters show his fierce countenance, as with an arresting pointing of his finger, he demands of his young listeners: "BE SOMEBODY!". In a similarly urgent but less direct and demanding way, the Spirit within us invites each of us to "BE SOMEBODY".

The primary gift to humankind, it seems, is this ability of ours to be aware and to expand our consciousness in space and time. We can strive to see more clearly, to understand better, and to know better the real values in this life, and based on that knowledge, to act wisely. We use our God-given minds, open to the promptings of God's Spirit, to search this out. The fruits of this effort, if we direct ourselves decisively, can be many wonderful things; some examples are those fruits that have been honored for centuries:

Charity, or a gaining of satisfaction from giving of ourselves, and helping others.

Joy, which is the ability to be uplifted in spirit, to see beauty and hope in the broader sphere, even in trying times.

Peace, that provides an inner calm in the knowledge that we're OK and secure in God's providence, despite threats to us; a satisfaction in doing what needs to be done; bringing peace to friend and foe alike, and even coping with violence in a non-violent manner.

Patience, with self-possession despite provocation; and a search for understanding of other's needs and the roots of other's problems or deficiencies.

Compassion for others, sharing in their joys and also in their difficulties and sorrows.

Fortitude, persevering with calm endurance, for the good of others; doing this even when we tire in a good cause, and our mettle is being tested.

Fidelity and trustworthiness, preserving personal integrity, and giving the respect that others deserve, even in the face of seductive allures.

Reverence, which includes respect and appreciation for the great beauty of all of God's creation, including our bodies and those of others.

To realize the existence of these opportunities, and to whole-heartedly resolve 'to be' by following this invitation of the Spirit within us, is, for some, like being born again. The exuberance of those who claim to be 'born again in the Spirit' is a puzzle and a source of suspicion for many observers. Yet, the phenomenon is evidently real. The inner joy in that pursuit, and the feeling of inner harmony, make that way of life seem almost like a different life. There's a 'dance of the spirit'. It's a life that joyfully partici-pates in the broader mission of 'birthing the Spirit of God' by spreading it around. It seems to us that every day of our lives we are given the opportunity to make this kind of choice, and so to be 'born anew' each day.

The human being thus appears to be a physical entity capable of holding and responding to the divine spark. Our similarity to God may be contained in this divine spark or spirit. That spirit motivates and enables a human being to seek persistently after further goodness, and to act responsibly for himself and for others. This creative spirit or energy within, it seems, seeks to reunite itself with the creative spirit from which it was drawn, and to form loving community with other like sparks.

John (1 Jn. 4:16-17) tries to express this concept of our growth to God, and the presence of God within us, when he says:

> God is love,
> and anyone who lives in love,
> lives in God,
> and God lives in him.

Thus, this spirit, acting within each of us, is one image, corre-sponding to an observed phenomenon, that is identified with the immanent presence and action of God. It is, some would say, the person of God acting in a human being; or, in other words, it is the work of the Holy Spirit, the third aspect of the Blessed Trinity. By it we participate in the process that is God. An awareness of this presence of the Spirit of God (sometimes buried), within every person, can have strong effects on our respect for one another, and on our mutual relationships. Perhaps more signifi-cantly, we can then recognize ourselves (and all other persons) as, in effect, a potential 'temple of God' and worthy of care and respect.

7.4 TOWARDS UNION WITH THE INFINITE

We also learn about God through the nature of his creation. Rosemary Reuther puts it this way:

> What we so easily forget in the world of plastic-wrapped food, electric light and electronic communication is that life is basically a freely given gift and that we are the great recipients of nature's grace. ... No matter how much we manipulate the gifts of the earth, ... ultimately we humans create nothing from nothing.[8]

If we can get away from our asphalt and concrete constructions, and get to a place where nature is still all around us, it's easier to be aware of the grandeur of that creation. We see the vastness of the cosmos with its millions of galaxies spread across millions of light years. We perceive the microcosm of the atom and the sub-atomic world, with it's own order and structures. We see the amazing complexity of our own bodies, such as the eye, - with it's ability to help us appreciate the beauty of a seaside sunset, the colors of a New England fall, or a Rembrandt painting. We realize that every breath we take is a miracle of sorts; we are sustained every second of our lives. All this is gift and a worthy cause for rejoicing and celebration. The wonderfulness of that total gift is the evidence of God's love. What image of God reflects this?

As we've discussed above, we are, in fact, parts of that vast evolving creation, - molecules, cells, plants, animals, and lastly the amazing humans, all of which forms a web of life stretching across time and around the world. Trying to filter out the short-term and dead-end sequences in that creation, we perceive a direction to that grand design, which leads to increasing complexity and consciousness. The human species is created capable of high awareness, consideration, and caring. The leading edge, in the evolution of that consciousness, is characterized by things like empathy, caring love, and kindness. We have ample evidence of their value in many men and women who have been willing to suffer greatly so that such goodness be maintained.

These noble traits indicate the direction of the design being created. Hence they also tell us something about that creator. They indicate the ultimate values of the designer. The nature of

God, then, may logically be the extrapolation of these qualities, which characterize the highest forms in the evolution of God's creation.

That image of God may require a quantum jump, to sets of superior characteristics we cannot fully comprehend, because we cannot really understand what we have not fully experienced. Our model of God is necessarily crude and incomplete, as we discussed before. It is simply the fullest reality of love that we can imagine. It is a type of personhood, of which the finest person we can imagine is only a dim reflection.

What mental images can serve to illustrate our relation to this loving reality that is beyond our faculties? Jesus expressed it in terms of a caring and kindly father-son relationship. Hence our familiar expression, "God, our Father". This is like a relationship between an elder and a younger, an "abba" or a wise and respected individual loving the younger, less experienced one. In another culture, a similar relationship might have been expressed as "God our Mother". Neither model can do justice to either the ultimate characteristics or the dedicated unity involved. We have, however, become accustomed to the "Our Father" concept, and it serves our purpose rather well.

We recognize the person of God, the creator of the universe, in this father-image. We associate our trust and dedication with it. There is little reason to question this image, but we should be open to other concepts, as well. For example, those who have had very poor relationships with earthly parents might better treat God as a person of infinite love, beyond the concepts of earthly father or mother.

We are in an on-going creation process, still incomplete, and involving our participation. We perceive our loving God to be yet active in that creation, and hence very much involved in our unfolding history. The process we perceive, then, is the very gradual movement of the human race towards these same ultimate, God-like characteristics.

The process involves our free-will decisions to promote and participate in that movement. The dedication of our lives to that direction amounts to a decision for unity with the author of that grand design. Our every decision, then, becomes a welcome opportunity to implement movement towards that unity. The alignment of our lives with that plan gives us a natural fulfillment, for it is in everyone's best interests, in the long run. This goal towards unity, through participation in the long-term evolution of consciousness, becomes the purpose and meaning of life.

Use of this second image of God, as Abba, recognizes our personal loving relationship to the creator, who wills our fulfillment as part of that on-going creation. From a sense of productive participation in this creative process, our lives gain meaning; we acquire self appreciation, hope, and confidence. Building on this, also, we can develop a greater degree of inner strength and tranquility.

7.5 THE EXAMPLE OF FULL UNITY

Many events contribute to the fabric of our understanding and inspiration. One life, however, now has a tremendous and unique effect on hundreds of millions of lives, around the globe. That is the life of the man called Jesus, who lived almost two thousand years ago. That event affected the course of history in very significant ways.

Jesus was a man, with a human-nature like the rest of men; but he was more. Like all others, he faced the temptations of worldly riches, the allures of power and authority, and the comforts of conformity. He chose, instead, a very different path. He succeeded in living fully with great love for all. His life, in words and actions, was a message, and an example of complete dedication to the fulfillment of God's apparent plan.

His life was an illustration of empathy, caring love, and kindness for friends and enemies alike. Forgiveness, and healing in spirit, mind, and body, were his constant activities. Respect was shown for every person, including the poor, the outcast lepers, the crippled, the scandalous sinners, and even the hated tax collectors. He related directly with the poor, talking, walking, eating with them. He reportedly had great sympathy for the sick, the lame, and the blind, and worked many healings. He lovingly recognized the dignity and worth of every person.

He did not teach dogma. Rather, he taught with imaginative parables, using images like: leaven, a lost coin, a mustard seed, etc., - more like a poet and an artist. By this means, he encouraged his listeners to think, and to discover something of the truth themselves. He frequently expressed his unity in spirit with God the Father, using the caring expression of "abba", loving parent.

With great inner strength, he was the advocate of the people against the abuses of the establishment. Courage and persistence in following this path, cost him his life, which he was ready to sacrifice, and great suffering, which he was ready to endure. His life and his cross have become signs and symbols of what fidelity to the plan of God means. It means choosing that way above all other ways, righteousness over expediency, the broader good over our own narrow pleasures. It involves a commitment to struggle for truth, peace, and justice. It means living as Jesus did and taking the consequences as he did, good and bad.

Thus, first of all, Jesus demonstrated the possibility of complete dedication of self to the love for God and one's neighbor. In this, therefore, it appears that Jesus is at least a prototype for the human species, as it moves towards unity with God. That prototype illustrates for all, the practical achievement of the goals of great empathy, caring love, kindness, and, above all, unity with the divine plan.

Secondly, he helped to verify a key hypothesis, - namely, that consciousness, in some form, persists after death. The actions of his love remained, not only from his memory, but in a real presence that was and is clear to his followers. The experience of that presence transformed the apostles from a state of great fear and confusion to confident and vigorous discipleship. Thus, Jesus, as the prototype, also strengthened the hope for the continuity of consciousness beyond current time. The purpose and meaning of life are therefore extended. The human person thus finds the opportunity to contribute not only a bit of consciousness during a lifetime, but also the creation of a consciousness that has continuity beyond. The resurrection of Jesus gives primary reinforcement to the hope of that continuity for all.

What are we to think of this man, Jesus, in the light of the above? This man, with a human nature, apparently succeeded in uniting his person with the ultimate design. As far as we know, this union was complete. He made visible the work of the ultimate architect. One can reasonably say that the Spirit of God was completely accepted by him, and that he welcomed the work of the Holy Spirit through him, without reservation.

Jung sees in Jesus the completion of the process of 'individuation', the realization of the self, the integration between the individual person and the universal God.[9] Both Rahner and the 'process theologians' see the incarnation of the word of God in Jesus as the full realization of what is the *potential*, the God-given, goal of all human beings.[10,11] In the life of Jesus, the process 'worked' completely.[12] While we each sense the spark, or the Spirit, of God within us, this Jesus was more. His, apparently, was a quantum jump in unity with God. We have, then, a concrete, real-life expression of God's nature, and a divine proto-type that we can relate to and aspire to work towards. Huston Smith writes:

> In the end, especially when he laid down his life for his friends, it seemed to those who knew him best that here was a man in whom the human ego had disappeared completely, leaving his life so completely under the will of God that it became perfectly transparent to that will. It came to the point where they felt that as they looked at Jesus they were looking at the way God would be if he were to assume human form.[13]

But, many ask, just exactly what was Jesus' relation to God, with whom this unity seemed so complete? Since God is relatively imperceptible to our finite minds, there is no way that an individual's own analysis can clarify this relationship very much. Still, what can we reasonably assume? It's interesting to note the range of popular expressions, acceptable to different groups, such as:

> a) Jesus was, in effect, a 'special messenger of God', one of a very small number in all of history who have served to illustrate the true nature of reality. Hence, he is a great teacher and prophet, the word of God, and the bringer of the gospel (as per Muslims and Bahai).

> b) Jesus' way is *the* way in which we can most profitably find personal fulfillment; and that way is a God-inspired means for greater unity with God; therefore he is a worthy focus of our entire lives. Jesus is, as his resurrection substantiates, now completely united with God. He is, therefore, an authoritative representation of God, and a dependable ex-pression of God (as per some 'liberal Christians').

> c) Jesus is, in human form, God's word and God's will, and thus God's son. Jesus is the revelation of the true reality of God, distinct from but one with the ultimate person we

regard as God our "Father" (as per 'more orthodox Christians').

Some Hindus would also accept (a) or (b), but add that other
persons in Eastern history also merit similar honors.
    While differences can be emphasized, there is also a very
substantial commonality that can lead to solidarity among the
holders of these widely held viewpoints. People holding a wide
range of beliefs are at least convinced that personal betterment
comes from a commitment to the way of life and the attitudes that
were taught and practiced by Jesus. In pursuit of that way, they
come closer to unity with God. Rather than rejecting any of these
positions, and separating ourselves from them, we prefer to
recognize them as fellow followers of Christ. We seek to be in
comradeship and communion with them. We, with several hundred million of these people, would add:

> In him we can clearly see God's spirit at work and in action.
> He is the tangible, living, expression of God's way. His prior
> example and, we believe, his present spirit, guide us and
> enliven us. In this way, he gives us new life. As our brother,
> whom we strive to emulate, he aids our quest for fulfillment,
> as we, too, strive for a greater unity with God. He is our
> constant friend and companion. He, therefore, is the focal
> point and the reference point in our lives.

Perhaps Monika Hellwig sums it up best when she says:

> As Christians, we see Jesus as the unique image of God in
> humanity. But we also see Jesus as prototypical and inclusive
> of us all, drawing us into His witness and His ministry of
> reconciliation and reconstruction, making us in union with
> Himself a kind a temple where God is to be encountered,
> experienced and brought to others by a royal priesthood.[14]

7.6 MERGING VIEWS FROM THE PAST AND THE PRESENT

These three images of God, the Holy Spirit acting within us, the
'Abba', Father of all creation, and the son of God, Jesus, prototype

for humankind, merge as three views and three expressions of a single reality. Each is meaningful in the process of humankind's evolutionary creation and our individual growth.

Traditional Views of the Birthing Process

Theologians have likened our participation in this whole process to a vast birthing of consciousness, and hence to a birthing of God himself. This is something one can barely comprehend. Many have tried with only little success. Some examples, however, help the concept. Meister Eckhart, the 14th century priest philosopher, has said:

> The seed of God is in us. If the seed had a good, wise, and industrious cultivator, it would thrive all the more and grow up to God whose seed it is, and the fruit would be equal to the nature of God.[15]

This approach to God by the human is somewhat clarified by Eckhart when he explains that we become God in the same way as a drop of water enters and becomes part of the sea.[16] Huston Smith states it differently, "It is as if an iceberg were suddenly to realize that it is H_2O."[17]

The continuous birthing, by each of us, of that interior spirit and way of living, so evident in Jesus, was also metaphorically expressed by Francis of Assisi. Referring to Jesus, the Christ (meaning Anointed One), Francis says:

> We are the mother of Christ when we carry him in our heart and body by love and a pure and sincere conscience. And we give birth to him through our holy works which ought to shine on others by our example.[18]

Teilhard makes a related point, saying "...the essential aspiration of all mysticism: to be united (that is, to become the other) while remaining oneself."[19] Teilhard further theorizes that the composing elements do not lose their individuality and particular character. The union is established by activities and functions, what we might call unity of purpose, rather than by unity of substance.[20]

These are all distinct but complementary expressions. They try to convey that we are intended to be 'of God', though we are

not God; that a part of us can be united with God, though no part
of us can be God.

Three Current Views of One Growth Process

In this light, everything we have been talking about in this book is
the one process of creation, of which we are still a growing part,
guided by and moving towards union with a Divine Providence.
That process of growth can be variously associated with the three
primary images of the one God:

> We human beings recognize the spark of God within us. We
> see the creative role we can play. We continuously mold our
> ideals and pursue them, striving for full personhood through
> growth in consciousness, under the urgings of the Holy
> Spirit.

> We see the inspiring example of Jesus, the full Son of God,
> the prototype for humankind, who fully lived the highest
> consciousness of caring love. This encourages us to emulate
> him, and to nurture our own potential to grow as he showed
> us, in order to become sons and daughters of God.

> We thereby strive to come into greater union with the
> benevolent force that guides all evolutionary creation. We
> broaden our consciousness to perceive the evolving grandeur
> of all creation, the work of 'Abba', our Father. We recognize
> the kinship of God in all of his creatures, particularly in the
> highest form, humankind.

7.7 THE UNIVERSAL RELIGIOUS KERNELS

Out of all this, can we find a few kernels that stand out in the
trajectory we called the world-wide growth of wisdom? Are there
a few essentials that are common to religions, in the East and the
West? We would hope that the following would be a plausible,
and perhaps acceptable, set of key concepts to many in different
faiths:

There is a single source of order in the universe and a corresponding guide to our destiny; this we associate with one Divine Providence. We sense and experience this Providence in creation and history. We are privileged to participate in this on-going creation of ourselves.

Our purpose is harmony and unity with the Divine Providence, and the Divine plan for humankind. A primary path to this unity is through decisive participation in the long-term growth of consciousness, - for example, empathy, caring love, and kindness. This growth of consciousness is our Divinely sponsored destiny, and ultimately fosters our fulfillment.

An inner force, or 'Holy Spirit', or 'seed of enlightenment', or 'the Spirit of God' acts within every person. This invites each to the pursuit of greater consciousness. As humans, we are able to discern that ideal; we are free to try to maximize the good in space and time, and hence to approach that ideal.

With an awareness of this loving Divine Providence, its action within each of us, and our potential for unity and harmony with it, we can acquire a profound sense of our own self worth.

A set of such fundamentals helps us all to foster solidarity with one another. We can hope together, as we 'follow our inner light'. We can expect that in so doing we are following a path that will lead to our unity with the Divine Providence. That doesn't require unity in symbolism or ritual but does require accepting each other, with our differences, in love. (Symbol and ritual, of course, are very helpful; the point is that they can be cultural and need not be uniform.)

Most practical, perhaps, is a focus on the 'way of life' that these principles espouse. Much of what we've addressed, in the way of personal fulfillment, is harmonious with the way taught by all of the great religions, especially as it has evolved in the scriptures. Each faith has its own expression of the optimum way, but they are mostly similar. Christians, many Muslims and some Hindus would see that special way as the one taught by Jesus; and many would add to the above:

Jesus responded, in an apparently complete way, to the invitation for unity with the Divine Providence. His alignment of his life in unity with the plan of God shows that unity to be a practical reality and an example for us.

The 'way' that he lived and taught reflected that unity with God, and provided us with a model that we can profitably and joyously emulate.

Perhaps one of the clearest expressions of that way is the "Prayer of St. Francis" which goes:

Lord, make me a channel of your peace;
Where there is hatred, let me sow love;
Where there is injury, pardon;
Where there is doubt, faith;
Where there is despair, hope;
Where there is darkness, light;
And where there is sadness, joy.

Divine Master, grant that I may not
So much seek to be consoled as to console;
To be understood, as to understand;
To be loved, as to love.

For it is in giving that we receive,
It is in pardoning that we are pardoned,
And it is in dying that we are born to eternal life.[21]

Followers of each of the great religions can find these basic sentiments of understanding and love in the teachings of their leaders. It seems evident that people in all cultures have been similarly searching for understanding, and evolving a common set of principles. Ministry to others in love and kindness is a common result.

Thus, it is not difficult to see the possibility of a divine spirit moving both East and West cultures towards a common understanding. Common ideas are propagated as the product is periodically pruned of additions which distract from the main direction. This commonality, we again suggest, is basically in the focus on growth of consciousness, which enables us to withstand the suffering and difficulties of life. That consciousness involves empathy, caring love, and hence, kindness to all in this life, forgiveness, healing of every kind of hurt, and a conscious, whole-hearted participation in the fulfillment of God's plan.

7.8 LIFE AFTER DEATH?

The hypothesis of some continuity of personal consciousness after death was strengthened by the resurrection event of Jesus, and by the very evident effects that followed. The Christian faith is built on the validity of Jesus' continued presence. This hypothesis of life after death not only gives a person hope for 'light at the end of the tunnel'; it also can give daily support through a sense of solidarity with persons in a common undertaking, both here and beyond.

We share a sense of comradeship, of common purpose, with people of good-will. Indeed, this comradeship cuts across many communities, and across many churches. It's apparent, on the other hand, that many church communities sometimes tend to view themselves as fortresses, who are in competition or even at war with one another. Sometimes a tribal mentality or just a sense of insecurity leads to triumphalism or a desire to be considered a solely-chosen people (rather than the notion that we are all chosen for some brand of service). Nevertheless, when churches are more successful in heightening their consciousness, - that is, their sense of empathy, love, and kindness, then the boundaries are some-what forgotten and their consciousness penetrates to the persons in other communities. That common comradeship might be re-ferred to as the 'Communion of Saints'. (Perhaps 'would-be-saints' would be a more appropriate name.)

That concept has been extended to also include those who have gone beyond this life and hopefully still maintain a comrade-ship with us. A faith in life hereafter prompts this sense of communion with those who may still be 'in the process of becoming' in a next life (some expect a time of further process in a state called 'Purgatory'), as well as with those who, we hope, have achieved a higher state of consciousness, in greater union with God. Thus the Communion of Saints can be an idea that joins together all those in the present who are striving for a higher existence and all those who went before us but still continue that process more or less closer to God.

The hypothesis is that their love, their consciousness, still exists and still is active in the community. Just as we are encouraged by the love of a friend, even though he/she is physically remote from us, so too we can feel supported by the love of all those who have gone before us. We are then, in communion with all the writers of the scriptures, and all those heroic persons who have helped to build our heritage, who hopefully consider us to be team mates in that grand construction.

Finally, the concept of life after death is an expression of the culmination of this evolutionary process towards greater consciousness. This culmination, the final Omega point, was described by the philosopher-scientist, Teilhard de Chardin. The Omega point, towards which the universe ultimately evolves, embraces all the consciousness which contributed to that evolution.[22]

The hope for participation in some such ultimate state spurs us on. The possibility of such a state, where the obstacles to full consciousness have been greatly eliminated, encourages us now to strive to overcome current obstacles.

Thus, the concept of the Communion of Saints stretches our consciousness in time, so that we relate to persons past, and we project our possible existence into the dim future. We establish a comradeship with like minded persons, both here and at our destination; and we gain hope of reaching a destination that promises continued fulfillment. So, again, this hypothesis of life after death, which is not unreasonable, also produces good results.

7.9 MIND IN UNION WITH GOD

We need to periodically withdraw a bit and find the space to pull ourselves together. It seems that our thoughts get stretched in different directions by pressures of the moment. At times distractions ricochet within our mind. There are many different procedures we can follow to reestablish a sense of quiet and central control, and to reaffirm our bearings and our desired direction. The practice of prayer does this, and more besides.

Consciousness tends to be narrowed by the pressures and urgencies of immediate needs. It takes a deliberate effort to spread one's consciousness, in space or time. Similarly, it takes a deliberate effort to stretch one's consciousness to the awareness of a reality beyond our senses, to the presence and caring of the Divine Providence. The effort is worthwhile, however, because the inclusion of God broadens our perspective and gives greater clarity and stability to it.

Prayer can be an integral and supportive part of our lives. Just living or reviewing our lives in the presence of God are forms of prayer. We hear about three major kinds of prayer: thanksgiving or praise, forgiveness, and supplication. Each can be adapted to harmonize with one's personal view of reality, and to reawaken that view with greater clarity. We try to illustrate that in the following.

Thanksgiving

Thanksgiving can be an expression of joy. The poorest peasant can rejoice daily in the incomparable gift of life, the air he breathes, the marvels of creation. We experience awe and beauty in the vastness of the stars and the majesty of mountains and rivers. We find still greater beauty in the delicateness of the opening flower, the song of the bird, and the sound of the rippling steam. And, once we learn to appreciate it, we find the greatest beauty and joy in the hearts of persons who have the ability to give of themselves for others. As Matthew Fox says:

> God is a gracious, an abundant, and a generous host/hostess. She has spread out for us a banquet that was twenty billion years in the making. A banquet of rivers and lakes, of rain and sunshine, of rich earth and of amazing flowers, of handsome trees and of dancing fishes.[23]

We can direct our consciousness not only to the beauty of nature, but also to the many gifts that come from it: our physical strengths and abilities, thinking, the arts of music, dance, or opera, constructive work, non-competitive sports, friendship, our sexuality, and the highest capabilities of empathy, caring love, compassion, and hospitality. Awareness of our gift of free choice and the opportunities we are given to create some good, as growing human beings, can add to that sense of gratitude and joy.

The song: "Praise God; praise him in the morning; praise him in the noon-time; praise him when the sun goes down," reflects that sense of continuous joy.[24] Prayers (and songs) of thanksgiving focus our awareness on the reality of our own beauty and that of the universe, even in its incomplete state.

Forgiveness

Asking forgiveness is an expression that seeks or affirms solidarity. It begins with a renewed attempt to perceive our possible place in the grand design, the kind of person we want to become, and the areas where we have been 'missing our target'. In this, we have to expand our awareness to include our relations with others, and the effects we have on their lives.

In the light of a broader consciousness, we focus on our fundamental bonds of comradeship with our fellow-persons, despite estrangements, and on our destined unity with the divine, despite distractions. We rekindle our awareness of the ever-present love of God, and of the divine urging to continue the work of consciousness growth. We reconsider what leads to our own true personal fulfillment. Reflecting on this, we try to understand the pluses and the minuses, particularly where we may have caused harm or loss to ourselves or others, so that 'mid-course corrections' may be in order.

In clearer view of the faith God has in each of us, we are moved to forgive ourselves also, and to move on. Seeking forgiveness prompts us to reopen the channels of cooperation that we may have closed. It concludes with a rededication and recommitment to the way that leads to this unity, - for Christians, a recommitment to the way that Jesus taught. It provides, then, a renewed sense of reconciliation and solidarity with the Divine Providence and with our 'brothers and sisters' that journey with us.

Supplication

Supplication is an expression of hope. Life is not continued sunshine, and can be filled with rain. Anxiety and suffering come, more or less, to all. Prayer, then, expands our awareness to the ever-present love of the Divine Providence, and draws hope for strength to pass through the darkness. Though not embracing suffering, we trust that any we endure will serve to build our strength, wisdom, and compassion, and draw us spiritually closer to God.

Our prayer illumines a trust in our ultimate destiny as full sons and daughters of God; we express our trust in the care of our 'Father', that will somehow lead us, and will give us what we need to carry on. We know that the best path is not necessarily the one that is most obvious to us; and we trust that in the broader Divine view, God will guide our path to a better end. We generate the hope that even from a present poor situation, God will help us to draw some good.

Humility

We're sometimes told that in conversing with God, we should have humility. That may sound demeaning; but it shouldn't be. The word humility comes from the word humus, - of the earth. We are one with all of creation. We depend on the plants for our food. We depend on the oxygen in the air. On the one hand, we rejoice in all the beautiful and wonderful gifts with which God has endowed us. On the other hand, we need to be realistic. In fact, we don't know it all; and we do need God's support in every breath we take. Amazing and beautiful though we may all be, we also recognize that we all are far from where we could be if we utilized all of our capabilities.

We need to recognize and accept our real limitations and our weaknesses. We need to trust that, despite these, the love that God has for us will result in our getting the strength to find harmony with God and our neighbor. This gift of hope inspires us to a renewed effort to achieve that of which we are capable. Realistically perceiving our place in God's plan, and buoyed by the expectation of his confidence in us, we hopefully and confidently recommit ourselves to full participation in that plan. We trust that God's love and wisdom, immeasurably beyond ours, will infuse our participation and will lead us ultimately to greater fulfillment.

Repetition

Repetition of prayer can be useless, a mere tranquilizer, or it can be a practical means for meditating on the reality beyond. It can be an occasion for heightening our awareness of our perceived reality. The network of thought prompted by seemingly rote prayer can be highly individualistic, can stretch our minds, and can reflect our current viewpoints. For example, consider the thoughts that might accompany the very familiar 'Our Father':

OUR FATHER - Jesus used the term, 'Abba', meaning a wise and deeply loving elder person; and this expresses our trust in a Divine Providence that guides our fabulous on-going creation;

WHO ART IN HEAVEN - existing within, throughout, and beyond our dimensions of space-time; in all the universe; wherever there is openness to God's spirit, and especially in the hearts of humankind;

HALLOWED BE THY NAME - including all the good that you stand for, the great drama of creation, and the benevolent plan you have for our fulfillment;

THY KINGDOM COME - your plan for our personal growth, and of humankind's fulfillment, come to fruition, with our hearty participation;

THY WILL BE DONE - we join our minds and hearts with yours, and commit our lives to the fulfillment of our destiny in your plan;

ON EARTH AS IT IS IN HEAVEN - so gradually a universal consciousness will pervade the earth; and the spirit of God will enliven every person;

GIVE US THIS DAY OUR DAILY BREAD - whatever we need to subsist and to grow spiritually in your love, within loving communities;

AND FORGIVE US OUR TRESPASSES - where we have misjudged what is best, or have missed our own targets;

AS WE FORGIVE THOSE WHO TRESPASS AGAINST US - helping to spread the spirit of God's forgiveness, hoping that they, too, will achieve personal fulfillment in God's plan;

AND LEAD US NOT INTO TEMPTATION - that might be more than we can cope with;

BUT DELIVER US FROM EVIL - by granting us the strength to cope creatively and hence to grow.

Thus, an idea benefits from being 'processed' in our minds. We turn it over and over, looking at it from different angles. Songs, too, help us to do this, as a tune carries us from verse to verse. With a relaxed mind, we explore the meaning of one thought after another. An example of this, that reexamines the message of God's patient empathy for us, is Betty's song, "The Willow Tree":

As I passed by, I saw a willow tree,
hanging tenderly, leaning yearningly,
above a stream that was bubbling merrily,
as it went rushing by, so heedlessly.

And as I passed, I thought I heard God speak to me.
He said, "You see that tree, as it hangs tenderly?
Just like that willow tree, I'm leaning over thee,
Oh, so lovingly, so protectingly--

Just like that willow tree, I'm yearning over thee
as you go rushing by, so heedlessly."

I thank thee God, for telling this to me.
I thank thee God, for all your loving me.
I thank thee God, for your protecting me,
as I go rushing by, so heedlessly.

As I pass by you, so unthinkingly,
I thank you God, for all your loving me.[25]

Focusing one's mind through repetition also can serve to help quiet the mind, set aside distracting 'noise', and empty ourselves of consuming desires. One is then in a better position to think clearly and seek further union with the cause of it all.

Meditation

A higher state of awareness of good, free from the pressure of distracting desires, is sought in the Eastern cultures by various forms of meditation. We're accustomed to a life of action; we seem to feel that we must be doing something, - accomplishing something. Meditation, on the other hand, is a quiet waiting, - for the inspiration and clarity that may be given to us.

A primary Eastern method for withdrawing, and actualizing our hidden infinite nature, is a training exercise called yoga. Yoga physical exercises, which relieve muscular tension, are often used in order to step by step bring the body to a quiet state. One seeks complete relaxation and balance of the body as a prelude to the relaxation and clarity of the mind. Silence is helpful as one lets go of all distractions. The mind is cleansed as all visual and cognitive images are allowed to drift away. As the body is brought to a relaxed state, the mind is also relaxed.

In Hindu meditation, the concentration of mind is to eliminate all external and internal distractions and to focus on nothing but the infinity which is God. This is said to finally bring a greater and greater awareness of God, awareness of the way to Godliness, and closeness to God.

Thomas Merton, in a letter to a Suffi scholar, describes his method of meditation (sometimes referred to as centering prayer) as follows:

> Strictly speaking, I have a very simple way of prayer. It is centered entirely on attention to the presence of God and to His will and to His love....One might say this gives my meditation the character described by the Prophet as "being before God as if you saw Him." Yet, it does not mean imagining anything, or conceiving a precise image of God, for to my mind this would be a kind of idolatry. On the contrary, it is a matter of adoring Him as all...My prayer is then a kind of praise rising up out of the center of Nothingness and Silence. ...It is not "thinking about" anything, but a direct seeking of the Face of the Invisible, which cannot be found unless we become lost in Him who is Invisible.[26]

Another object of meditation may be 'the Way of God in Ourselves', seeing ourselves experiencing the Godlike qualities we seek after. Meditations might be, for example, on the subjects of mercy, forgiveness, and compassion, or the seven gifts of the Spirit mentioned above, such as charity, peace, patience, or fortitude. Another sequence, in Eastern practice, might focus on equanimity, detachment, truthfulness, serenity, or quiet courage. Dwelling quietly on each subject, our minds settle down, shake out the jangling pieces, and focus objectively on the quality we seek. In time, the realization of the quality becomes clearer, and a more integral part of ourselves.

Thus, the various forms of prayer, - thanksgiving, forgiveness, supplication, or meditation, can be powerful means for consciousness raising. Sometimes, prayer prompts joy, renewed solidarity, or hope. Sometimes, it simply heightens awareness of our identity, of the paths to real personal fulfillment, and of our relation to God. In each case, prayer can be a powerful mind expanding experience.

7.10 THE PERSONAL COMMUNION

Perhaps one of the most widely used forms of prayer is what is known as 'holy communion', or the Eucharist. It combines a physical sign of union with an interior dedication. Unique to Christians, the Eucharist is often incomprehensible to others; misunderstood, it even seems to be a source of scandal to some. As the central act of liturgy for many, we suggest that it, too, is a key practice in the raising of consciousness.

As humans, we are able to think in the abstract, quite separated from the corresponding physical objects. That is one of humankind's unique strengths. For example, the basic concepts of empathy and caring love can be considered quite abstractly. Nevertheless, it is often a physical expression of the abstract that is needed to aid our comprehension of it. Physical symbols and signs (for example, the flag, and the heart-symbol) are often used to help achieve this comprehension. To us, the Eucharist is a truly remarkable example of a physical sign of an abstract concept and a profound reality. The following is an attempt to convey our personal view of this extremely important event. It reflects our personal experience, without any attempt at dogmatic definition.

The Eucharist makes no sense at all without at least some basic faith. Two planks seem to us to be key:

First, it is our faith that God is not merely present in the world, but that a spark of God can 'live' in every person. That presence can be nurtured to become a greater part of a person's life.

This presence 'lives' to the extent that the person decisively joins in attempting the fulfillment of the divine plan. It is evidenced, for those with that faith, in the practice of consciousness for others despite their deficiencies. As discussed above, Jesus apparently succeeded fully in this, cooperating completely in the divine will.

Second, as Jesus also verified by his teaching and by his own continued presence, we believe in the continuation of some form of consciousness after death.

These two concepts: the movement of each person toward unity with the divine consciousness, and the continuity of consciousness after death, provide the backdrop to the dramatic concept of the Eucharist. Jesus is reported to have said "Take this and eat; this is my body, which shall be given up for you.", and "Take this and drink; this is my blood which shall be shed for you; do this is memory of me." What can it mean to a Christian who repeats this scenario in memory of him? Of course, like everything else, it may mean absolutely nothing to the unthinking person. But to one who is at least partially aware of the above two concepts, it can be most meaningful and consciousness - raising.

The sharing of the bread and the wine, as he instructed, is the physical sign of the unity that is sought. This sign of unity, accompanying the act of stepping forward to be in union, then provides a setting for a renewed commitment to the way taught by Jesus. It encourages a total commitment, as Jesus made a total commitment. The acts of eating and drinking dramatically emphasize the point that the 'essence' of the person, Jesus, is united with our person. That's a most dramatic idea. His consciousness joins with ours and strengthens our consciousness, as real food does for our bodies. The physical sharing heightens the sense of comradeship between each person and Jesus, who gave his life in the common cause of fulfilling the divine plan.

Zakhor, the Hebrew word for 'remember', means more than mere remembering; it also means 'to act'.[27] Jesus' call is to act as he has acted. In response, one can have a renewed commitment to his way. Fr. John P. Egan expresses the remembrance well:

There was the bread and wine sharing. For Jesus, it symbolizes the sharing of body and blood, a willingness to be broken and bleed for the sake of love and reconciliation. "Do this in remembrance of me," Jesus pleads to the gathered and to all who will gather together through the ages. Serve, love, share life at risk of dying. It is a call to vulnerability, an invitation to all to remember the way Jesus lived and loved and tried to be priest by returning us to the circle of communion, by reconnecting us and making us whole.[28]

Most Catholics would express the event more in terms of an intimate communion with the divine. The Eucharist prayer says: "Through Jesus, with Jesus, and in Jesus, and in union with the Holy Spirit, all glory and honor is given to you, almighty Father". A dominant thought can be that since Jesus is completely united with God, the Father, then, communion with Jesus, the son of God, amounts to union with God, the Father.

In any case, this physical and decisive action in memory of Jesus, has proven to be remarkably effective, for the thinking person. It provides a means for focusing one's attention on the spiritual, emphasizing the idea of Christ's empathetic spirit present in one's self and in others, recommitting one's life to a particular direction, and achieving a certain sense of unity, through Jesus, to the Father.

When the individual is truly in communion with the way of life taught by Jesus, and through him in communion with the being of God, then the person is more disposed to forming living community with those around. In his life and in his death, Jesus offered his body and his blood, his entire being, in the service of God and humanity. The Eucharist is an occasion for the follower of Jesus to associate directly with that mode of living. The follower thus is motivated to offer his or her own body and blood, - that is, the very essence of one's being, likewise in the service of others and hence in the service of God. At the same time, it is a comradeship and a joining of one's commitment with that of all others sharing the same Eucharist. As Teilhard said:

All communions of all men, present, past and future, are one communion.[29]

One can have a sense of one's total being, - mind, inner spirit, and body, united, along with others, in this 'way' of Jesus. The Eucharist thus becomes not only a commitment to God, and to the way taught by Jesus, and to others, but also, thereby, a commitment to one's own inner fulfillment.

Remembering this person who lived two thousand years ago, remembering the way he lived, and resolving to orient our lives in that direction, we stretch our minds in space and time, and beyond space time. The early Christians thus sought to *be with* the spirit of Jesus, to live in his way, and with him to accept *interiorly* the Spirit of God. In a sense, then, they sought a more active role with God, as adopted 'sons and daughters' of God. Paul wrote (Galatians 4:6-7):

> The proof that you are sons is that God has sent the spirit of his Son into our hearts: the spirit that cries, "Abba, Father," and it is this that makes you a son, you are not a slave any more; and if God has made you a son, then he has made you heir.

With this type of awareness, we begin to comprehend the possibility of a fulfillment of the words of Jesus promising his presence in us (John 15:5):

> I am the vine,
> you are the branches.
> Whoever remains in me, with me in him,
> bears fruit in plenty;

7.11 PROOF OF THE PUDDING

Thus, our position, today, can stem from a fully aware and searching faith. We can be comfortable with renewed insights on the traditional images of God. We can see in all of this the unfolding idea of the birth of God's spirit in the hearts of humankind. We can move towards greater comradeship with God, in various forms of prayer and communion. However, all this has meaning only if it affects our daily lives in practical ways. "The proof of the pudding is in the eating."

As each of us gradually absorbs the way of thinking and acting that consciousness promotes, we resolve to use our free will to join in that campaign of striving for birth. We do that, in everyday life, by an appropriate emphasis on empathy, caring love, and kindness. By growing ourselves, we add our bit to the growth of God's spirit in the world.

This consciousness effects a person's approach to everything, - such as suffering, forgiveness, opportunities for community, and the challenges of wealth, sex, and authority. We each can further participate in that grand process of creation as we work to overcome separatisms and social injustices, which inhibit this growth process. We can reap some small measure of the gifts of the Spirit, such as inner peace, patience, compassion, and fortitude. We can gain a healthy reverence for all of God's creation.

In short, we each can choose to participate imaginatively, by our conscious decisions, in the continuous birthing of the Spirit of God in the 'hearts' of humankind. We discover, to our delight, that in this way we find the beginnings of great satisfaction, joy, and fulfillment.

REFERENCES

[1]Andrew Greeley and Mary Greeley Durkin, *How to Save The Catholic Church*, Viking Penguin Inc., N. Y., 1984, pp. 18–22.

[2]Matthew Fox, *Original Blessing*, Bear & Co., Santa Fe, New Mexico, 1982, p. 90.

[3]Andrew Greeley and Mary Greeley Durkin, *loc. cit.*, p. 41.

[4]Norman Pittenger, *Christology Reconsidered*, SCM Press, London, 1970, p. 141.

[5]Norman Pittenger, *God In Process*, SCM Press, London, 1967, pp. 19–20.

[6]Paul F. Knitter,*No Other Name?*, Orbis Books, Maryknoll, N.Y., 1985, p. 25.

[7]Karl Rahner, "Observations on the Concept of Revelation", *Revelation and Tradition*, Herder and Herder, N.Y., 1966, pp. 9–25.

[8]Rosemary R. Reuther, "It's Unnatural to Dominate Earth", *National Catholic Reporter*, Sept. 27, 1985, p. 32.

[9]Carl Jung, *Psychology and Alchemy*, Collected Works of Carl G. Jung, vol 12, Roatledge and Kegan Paal, N.Y., 1953, p. 19.

[10]Karl Rahner, *Sacramentum Mundi*, vol 3, p. 195; *Theological Investigations*, vol.1, p. 187; *Foundations*, pp. 193–195.

[11]Norman Pittenger, *God In Process*, SCM Press, London, 1967, pp. 19–20.

[12]Paul F. Knitter, *loc. cit.*, pp. 190, 192.

[13]Huston Smith, *The Religions of Man*, Harper and Row, New York, 1958, p. 310.

[14]Monika K. Hellwig "A Royal Priesthood", *America* May 9, 1987, p. 393.

[15]Meister Eckhart, *Breakthrough: Meister Eckhart's Creation Spirituality in New Translation*, Introduction and Commentaries by Matthew Fox, Doubleday & Company, Inc., Garden City, New York, 1980, p. 512.

[16]*Ibid.*, p. 319.

[17]Huston Smith, *Forgotten Truth*, Harper and Row, New York, 1977, p. 91.

[18]Matthew Fox, *Ibid.*, pp. 221–222.

[19]Teilhard De Chardin, *The Divine Milieu*, Harper Torchbooks, N.Y., N.Y., 1965, p. 116.

[20]Beatrice Bruteau, *Evolution Towards Divinity*, The Theosophical Publishing House, Wheaton, Ill., 1974, p. 82.

[21]Saint Francis of Assisi, 1182 - 1226, founder of the religious order of Friars Minor, usually known as the Franciscans.

[22]W. Henry Keney, *A Path Through Teilhard's Phenomenon*, Pflaum Press, Dayton, Ohio, 1970.

[23]Matthew Fox *ibid.*, p. 112.

[24]Song "Praise God, praise Him in the morning", author unknown.

[25]copyright by Cora Elizabeth Cypser, 1988.

[26]M. Basil Pennington, *Thomas Merton, Brother Monk*, Harper & Row, Publishers, San Francisco, 1987, pp.160–161.

[27]Mathew Fox, *Ibid.*, p. 304.

[28]John P. Egan: "The 'Hood' is the Problem With Priesthood", *National Catholic Reporter*, April 19, 1985.

[29]Teilhard De Chardin, *The Divine Miliew*, Harper Torchbooks, N.Y., N.Y., 1965, p. 124.

8

GOING TO WORK

Going forth each day builds on the work of all previous days. Yet, each day is another challenge, and another opportunity. The possibility is there to make each encounter an occasion for growth, - growth in our own consciousness. If we can keep a broad enough perspective, we have a chance of seeing the sacramentality - the occasion for God's grace - in every event of our daily lives. With a little discipline, then, we have a good chance of getting satisfaction and enjoyment out of life.

8.1 THE INCENTIVE TO CHANGE

Humankind *can* be conscious, but at present, it seems obvious that most of us still live below our legitimate level. It is still very common for people to live in the power of negative emotions, and negative illusions, as they deceive themselves and harbor negative attachments. The result is a relatively constrained and narrow existence.

Each person does, however, have the power to change and to grow himself or herself.[1] Each of us can be more conscious or more asleep, more divided or more whole. We can deceive ourselves more or less, yield more completely to mechanicalness

Figure 8: Each of Us Chooses His Own Path
Despite Obstacles, Suffering, and Setbacks

or less, indulge in fewer negative emotions or be immersed in negative emotions.

The incentive to change and grow comes from the realization of our present situation and of the possibility of change. It is the realization of having been asleep, of inner divisions, negativeness, and the unpleasantness of such things that gives one the impulse to change.[2] Incentive also comes as we realize that it is possible to know more about ourselves. As we begin to acquire certain knowledge, new possibilities of understanding and growth open up.

However, wanting is not achieving. If we want something we must pay for it with effort. Consciousness cannot be given; it can only be developed by training, practice in overcoming obstacles, and refusal to let defeats be permanent. Repeated failures must be accepted as learning experiences, with a belief that gradually we will improve.

More than that, we must each strive to make some contribution towards 'building the earth'. The construction of a new civilization must be moved at least a little bit forward by each of us. That civilization must ultimately foster the dignity of all, as children of our common God and co-creators with him. Even small progress along these lines must be earned by work and if necessary by pain and suffering.

Even so, that work and pain can also have a bit of creative delight. The joy of building the earth can be shared and celebrated by all, as we all use our inherent creativity and artistry in our daily lives. That creativity is the flower of the seed of consciousness that God has placed in us. Working and sacrificing for the continuous birthing of consciousness, we can build ourselves, and we can build the earth.

8.2 CONSCIOUSNESS TRAINING

Training by the athlete is taken for granted as a necessity. However, in our ordinary lives, training is often shunned and considered an unnecessary burden. Nevertheless, we know from experience that to excel in anything demands training. The development of consciousness is no exception.

Refreshing Our Goals

First, it would seem that our goals and ideals need to be periodically re-examined, reformulated, and refreshed; and we need to practice explicitly placing these goals near the foreground of our thought in every situation. Some, for example, would simply emphasize a 'fundamental option' for God's justice in respect to the poor and the oppressed. As is abundantly evident in this book, we find value in a focus on the words 'empathy, caring love, and kindness'. In this, or some similar way, it helps if each person's goal is periodically reformulated, stated concisely, and frequently remembered.

Building Muscle

Once each person has shaped his or her own set of ideals, the job has just begun. One must regularly reinforce adherence to those ideals by some form of training. All kinds of techniques have been tried so as to discipline the entire self towards some higher goals. Let's look at some examples of techniques that have been used, some for a very long time.

1. Appetite Control

We need to see ourselves as being in control of ourselves. In general, satisfying selfish desires seems to result in a corrosion of consciousness. Self denial of selfish satisfaction, on the other hand, strengthens will power, and further establishes the identity of the person. Self control requires a readiness to 'take control of the steering wheel' of our lower level mechanisms, and to steer them into productive channels. Therefore, the control of the bodily appetites has long been a favorite means of training the person.

Fasting and abstinence from food, for example, have been an accepted way of developing self control. Today, this might also be a discipline of eating and drinking sensibly, and doing without on occasion. Eating less meat and sweets, for example, also turns out to be more healthy.

Offering up even little sacrifices in the interests of someone in need, builds comradeship and a healthy spirit. A little fast, or doing without some comforts, and use of the money, instead, to feed the starving, is a regular ritual for some. Any bit of discipline, in performing some regular acts of compassion or kindness, is vastly sweeter if the empathy and caring are genuine. What would be the effect on someone seriously ill in the hospital, or in prison, if you told them you would fast and pray for their intention? It could have a seemingly magical effect.

Such regular little disciplines seem to allow a higher level of consciousness to flourish. It trains us to control the impulses of the child in us. Control of other appetites, such as sex, or a lust for power, also benefit from a comparable discipline. In each case, sensible enjoyment, deferment when that is in the best interests of others, and a willingness to serve others rather than only ourselves, brings deep and lasting satisfaction.

Such discipline is needed if we are to set each use of an appetite into a higher context. Should not each enjoyment of a God-given appetite be appreciated as one of God's wonderful gifts? How often, too, can that enjoyment be accompanied by a caring attitude for another? When these apply, the human capability for consciousness transforms the situation from a purely selfish satisfaction of appetite, to being part of a larger and nobler purpose. Enjoyment of an appetite thus can be a means to a higher end, rather than merely an end in itself.

2. Withdrawal and Reflection

Withdrawing to a quiet state, in general, enables one to collect and develop one's awareness. Huston Smith sees in Buddha's life the same pattern which Toynbee found basic to creativity in all history, the pattern of 'withdraw and return':

> Buddha withdrew for six years, then returned for forty-five. But each year was similarly divided; nine months in the world, the rainy season spent in retreat with his monks. His daily cycle, too, was patterned to this mold; his public hours were long, but three times a day he withdrew, that through meditation he might restore his center of gravity to its sacred inner pivot.[3]

We all need periodic intervals of withdrawal to keep our balance. However, in our hurried lives, these are all too rare. In addition, we need to find moments for brief periods of reflection. In short times of recollection, and then in brief flashes during every difficulty, we can just 'remember ourselves'.[4] We need to very simply remember who we are, what our basic purpose is, and what our primary methods are. For example, what would be the effect, if each of us remembered, frequently, that:

I am a beloved child of God.
There is a tiny 'spark of God' within me.
I can grow in consciousness;
I will be increasingly empathetic, caring, and kind.
I visualize myself growing in this way.

Whatever the method, some practice of periodic withdrawing to a quiet state, however brief, and reflecting on the way of living that we desire, builds strength to pursue that way.

3. Regular Prayer

Frequent, periodic prayer can also be an effective discipline and training in consciousness. It is the backbone, for example, of life in many monastic communities. It is also effectively used by many Muslims in everyday life. Prayer five times a day is, for them, mandatory. Frequency of prayer, it seems, is indeed valuable, but quality of prayer, that promotes consciousness, would seem to be an essential ingredient.

Perhaps the simplest, and the most-widely used, practice of all is the brief, daily, prayer, upon awaking in the morning and before going to sleep at night. This can involve a simple reformulation of the kind of person we want to become, some consideration of ways to achieve that, and recommitting the day to that path. Aligning that resolution with what we perceive to be God's plan (or, for example, with the way of living and of treating others that Jesus taught), adds a foundation to that commitment.

Mealtime, too, can be a convenient occasion to pause a moment, reflect on the vast beauty of creation, remember the good of which people are capable, thank God for all her gifts, and rededicate ourselves to our chosen direction.

Thus, by daily prayer, with daily redirection, at regular points during the day, we can quiet ourselves and steer our course. Is this not a practical way to steadily shape our identity and move towards what we want to become?

4. Periodic Assessment

Still another ancient practice is that of periodic, overall, assessment of how one is doing. The sacrament of reconciliation in the Catholic Church, is an example of this.[5] In general terms, we each have a set of targets for how we want to live, - for example, the ideals we spoke of earlier. If we periodically assess our hits and misses, we can systematize our mid-course corrections. We can, on these occasions, reconsider what our most important targets really are, reflect on why we tend to deviate from them, and decide where particular efforts must be made to achieve our goals. Keeping a positive outlook, we can focus on the *improvements* we project, in our capability and our behavior, the next time we encounter similar circumstances. It helps if we see our future selves, in our minds, more nearly achieving our goals.

The process is made more effective by involving a need for reconciliation or even repayment where either is appropriate. The process can also involve performing some specific act of discipline or charity (penance) to give a concrete form to the resolutions made.

Thus, a periodic and thorough 'taking stock', assessing the good and the not so good, can help in redirecting our longer range direction and plans. It also can be the occasion for sinking our roots deeper where we want them, finding reconciliation with our neighbor, ourselves, and our God, and strengthening the alignment of our course with what we perceive to be God's plan for us.

5. Personal Plans

These days, few that we know of are willing to follow someone else's requirement for a training regimen. Whether it's dieting, getting off smoking, or building biceps, no outside pressure is likely to be effective for long. The only way most of us are going to train is if we ourselves decide positively to do it, no matter what. So, too, with consciousness training. The right blend of things like appetite control, quiet reflection, self remembering, regular prayer, and periodic reassessment, must be a personal crusade. A private practice must be tailored to each one's needs and inclinations. Each of us is the only one who can build discipline into himself.

Laws, Punishment, and Rehabilitation

In our society, as in many others, there is a presumption that the greater good can be promoted through an intricate set of laws and regulations. This would be especially productive if these were guidelines, which resulted from the accumulated wisdom of prior generations, on how the community as a whole can best obtain fulfillment. In part, this goal is achieved, - for example by laws which protect human rights. In other areas, however, it seems that our society has developed a questionable maze of general and special-interest laws. Much of this pertains to property laws which protect those that have, from those that have not.

We increasingly resort to imprisonment of those who violate these laws. In theory, this is not solely for punishment, but also an inducement to re-examination, a change of heart, and a rehabilitation of the offender. The opportunity for retraining on the higher levels of consciousness, is supposedly there. The very high recidivism rate, however, does not indicate much success in that regard. Threat of punishment has proven to be an expensive failure as a means of deterrence or reconstruction.

On the other hand, some volunteer-sponsored programs, distinct from the correctional institutions, do seem to have significant rehabilitation effects. Among these are the Alternatives to Violence program (sponsored by the Quakers), the New Directions program, Alcoholics Anonymous, and some religious-sponsored programs such as the Residents Encounter Christ weekends. All of these emphasize consciousness raising, and training in the application of consciousness.

These prison programs demonstrate that an individual heals himself more readily in an environment of love and caring from others, which builds self respect. The experience of participating in a concerned community provides the catalyst that enables the interior actions of healing oneself. Another quality of an effective training program is that it forms a community in which all the participants succeed in giving of themselves for the cause of the others.

The bottom line is that a) punishment, in itself, does not work and b) fostering consciousness, and bringing out the best that is in every person, heals and rebuilds better than any other process.

Enjoying the Pursuit

Thus, over many centuries, humankind has tried to devise a wide range of approaches and exercises to help develop and train the higher levels of consciousness. One must grudgingly admit that only with a deliberate and systematic practice of some sort can we expect to excel in our own development.

An essential ingredient, we're convinced, is a sense of

creativity and a voluntary pursuit of excellence. There's work involved, allright, - lots of it; and the continued effort requires some discipline. However, think about any artist, piano player, or athlete; won't they tell you that the pain of the labor is forgotten in the joy of anticipating the goal? The ultimate objective must have a great attraction if the effort is to be inspired and not just mechanical. If developing our consciousness, - empathy, caring love and kindness, is really the first purpose in our lives, then that attraction will be there, and a systematic pursuit of consciousness will be a pleasure.

8.3 GRABBING HOLD DESPITE MISFORTUNE

Life can be beautiful; but many know that it also can be depraving, demeaning, abusing, and even despairing. We sometimes need to use all of our available resources to make progress against that tide.

At times, we forget that we each have unending potential for development. In fact, we limit our own growth by locking onto an image of ourselves that is less than our potential. The put-downs of others, the disappointments, and the failures, are allowed to create a greatly diminished image of ourselves. Then, our subconscious leads us to perform, almost automatically, in fulfillment of that distorted image.

We need to recognize this, and work constantly to create a more beautiful image of ourselves, - one intended by God, - not one imposed by others or earlier events. We can do this by deliberately thinking positively about the future. We can 'see' an image of ourselves as we are becoming, - as if it already is. That way, we dispel the distorted image.

Misfortune and personal diminishment must not be allowed to totally impede us. Rather than letting our minds be darkened by things that we suffer, we must remain determined. No matter what happens to us, we must try to remain steadfast, immovable, and determined to maintain hope, and even to generate thoughts of compassion and good will.

We each learn as we live, and even profit from our misfortunes. We learn that we can live with dignity, despite circumstances or the past. We find that some things are much more important than others. We find we can still treat all others with understanding, kindness,and respect, and try to help the disadvantaged, wherever we encounter them. With self possession, we can affirm all others, rather than pointing out their weaknesses. With a sense of humor, we can promote harmony rather than discord. With attention to good communication, we can cooperate in efforts for our mutual good. Despite our surroundings or setbacks, then, we can gradually become full persons, as we were destined by God to be.

With goals clearly in mind, let us try to be grateful for every small improvement in ourselves. We can recognize and celebrate every good point we possess, and steadily build confidence in ourselves. Being mindful of God's presence at all times, we can know we are loved and forgiven, and have great value in his sight.

Thus, despite great personal tragedy, people are able to see the overall goodness of God. They still can see their continuing role, as co-creators with God, of good in the world. With that vision, they can grab hold of their deepest selves and determine to live fully and joyfully.

8.4 ACTION GUIDELINES

Building upon a foundation of a personal ideal, and reinforced by consciousness training, each one of us can benefit further by some set of action guidelines. Different cultures and action groups formulate guidelines with varying emphasis, but again, there is much in common.

Look at some of the well known guidelines. Many simply rely on the basic Ten Commandments of the Old Testament (prohibitions and their opposites, as in section 6.6). Boiling it all down, Jesus said, of the two Great Commandments, "Love the Lord your God with all your heart, and with all your soul, and with all your mind. And a second is like it, you shall love your neighbor as yourself" (Matthew 22:37). (That surely implies that we should also love ourselves!) In the Orient, the Eightfold Path of Buddha, has been widely followed. An example of more specialized guidelines is the use of Transforming Power in the Alternatives to Violence Project.

The Eightfold Path of Buddha

Buddha prescribed his Eightfold Path[6,7] as a course of training. One can find here a disciplined pursuit of greater consciousness.

The preliminary step is right association, since we are influenced constantly by the examples, attitudes, and values of our companions. Then there is the deliberate striving, every day, for:

1. Right Knowledge - realizing that suffering abounds, that it is occasioned by drives for selfish existence, gnawing desire, greediness, and covetousness; and that the means to its cure is the Eightfold Path.

2. Right Aspiration - setting for ourselves some ideals that oppose separateness, selfishness, greed, and anger, and outlining a map of how we are to achieve these ideals; focusing our energies, with sure and constant determination, to pursue our ideals, and identifying ourselves with the welfare of all.

3. Right Speech - to be always constructive, and to search for the motives that prompt any lack of charity in what we say; avoiding belittling, tactlessness, and poisonous wit; avoiding lying words, abusive words, and double tongues.

4. Right Behavior - to be selfless and charitable, understanding our behavior, and the motives which prompt it; reflecting on the kindliness or self-seeking of the things done; changing to the better direction.

5. Right Livelihood - using our time and energy in occupations that promote life and awareness, instead of inhibiting them.

6. Right Effort - exerting ourselves enormously, with will power, in a steady pull to achieve the better direction, and the goal of enlightenment.

7. Right Mindfulness - keeping our mind in control of our senses, instead of allowing the latter to become Lord; remembering who we are; being steadily aware of what we are doing; picturing vividly our desired goals; and pervading the world with loving thoughts for all creatures.

8. Right Absorption - keeping the mind tranquil, so as to tap inner strengths, and to perceive the beauty of true reality, free from frantic desires.

Many millions of people in the East, for centuries, have found these guidelines to be a useful basis for the conduct of their lives. Yet, none of these ideas is strange to the Western mind. Isn't it interesting, that we, here, can find such comradeship and common purpose with all those of such a different culture?

Transforming Power

The opposite of using advanced consciousness would seem to be resorting to unnecessary violence. Yet we frequently encounter it, and must learn to cope with it. Violence is any deliberate, destructive action against a person. There are, evidently, many forms of violence in the world today. Some are physical, cultural, mental or psychological. They range from common put-downs and lack of respect, to murder. They affect every person's life.

Confrontation of such evil is just as important as the promotion of good. However, the method of confrontation can itself promote either good or evil in the form of unnecessary violence. We usually make only a little effort in a search for a solution to such violence. Failing to find a quick solution, there frequently is a tendency to resort to another violence in order to alleviate the first. Monika Hellwig analyzes the problem as follows:

> ... this leaves all the usual factions, oppressions, class distinctions, national hostilities, and so forth in place as before. Indeed, by these means hostilities, suspicions and exclusions seem to intensify and proliferate. To actualize God's reign among us, with all that means, obviously requires something more. It requires gestures of reconciliation that seem to run counter to common sense and prudence. It requires us to overcome anger, hostility and suspicion in others, not by retaliation and restraint of their power to act, but by a kind of de-escalation or defusing.

Actual historical experience suggests that people who are violent and abusive act out of grievances, real or imagined, and never really think the score has been evened when their violence has been reciprocated. Therefore, violence tends to spiral indefinitely and to escalate.[8]

Much violence has an underlying cause, - if only we can discern it. Anger and hatred, for example, may have their roots in feelings of helplessness, inadequacy, unworthiness, and loneliness.[9] A feeling of oppression may be from obvious or very subtle factors. The remedy may be in reducing the factors which create helplessness, or in changing the attitude of the oppressed. Anger diminishes markedly when resentment is removed. Loving the oppressor (while working for his change), may be possible. A prerequisite to that, in turn, may be the confidence of the oppressed he is in fact also loved, - loved by his God.

Raising one's consciousness, and practicing empathy, caring love, and kindness, may sometimes seem theoretical in the face of real life situations. It can, however, be used in a very practical manner. As one example, Transforming Power is a process that is advocated by Quaker groups[10] and is admirably harmonious with the concepts of promoting increased consciousness and a sense of community. Their activity is called the Alternatives to Violence Project (AVP). The essential guidelines of this program that have been found to be very practical by many prison inmates and others, are as follows:

1. Empathy

Remember that the adversary is a fellow human being. Try to put yourself in the opponent's shoes, and to realize why he feels and acts the way he does. Discern what the needs of the opponent are.

Approach each conflict with the belief that your opponent has something in him (perhaps hidden) that wants to do what is right. Constantly try to reach that 'something'.

Seek to establish a degree of trust. Put the adversary more at ease, with less to fear. Only then can issues be examined more dispassionately.

Listen to the adversary. Everyone has made a journey. Try to understand where the other person is coming from before you make up your mind.

Allow the sincere views of all parties to mingle. Advance ideas tentatively at first, letting them be exposed to the conscientious different views of others.

Avoid the fatal tactics of trying to convey an image of your superiority. Don't threaten or put-down; simply show courage and strength, instead.

2. Searching

Define the problem in terms of the needs of each opponent, - including the feelings, motives, and other needs which prompt the behavior of each party.

Generate as many possible alternative solutions as are feasible.

Search for the 'win-win' combinations, where each party can fulfill their basic needs.

Search for ways to surprise the opponents, as with humor, as this promotes rethinking.

Constantly reexamine your own position to make sure it is true, fair, and considerate of others. If not, quickly revise it without trying to save face.

3. Perseverance

As long as your position is true, fair, and considerate of others, expect to experience great inward power to support it without fear. Be ready to follow the leading of that power, acting boldly, courageously, and even dangerously (though non-violently), if so led.

If reason fails, stand firm in support of basic principles. This firm stand must then be a force able to withstand all opposition. The force of a just cause, that is long upheld, will eventually dissolve prejudice and selfishness.

Do not welcome hardship or suffering; but your goals or principles may be so vital that you must be willing to suffer physically or mentally to achieve them. When this happens, your acceptance of the necessary suffering can change your adversaries and win allies to your cause.

Draw sustaining power from the belief that non-violent persistence in a just cause, with continuing respect for your adversary, is the only truly constructive and successful approach in the long run.[11]

The folks that teach the techniques of achieving the above rely on basic and simple ideas. A wide range of exercises and games is used to teach self respect, respect for others, communication skills, cooperation, empathy, and trust. For example, one of the very elementary disarming exercises is to show respect for your adversary by simply listening to him. As a matter of fact, listening when under stress turns out to be an art that is little practiced by most. The good listener is involved with and empathizes with the speaker, and frankly opens himself to the possibility of being changed by what he hears. The good listener reassures the speaker by conveying back understanding of what he has heard. Somehow, he signals that he understands where the other person is coming from.

Understanding the feelings of our adversary is only half the picture. The other half is conveying how we feel, but doing this without denunciation or escalating the conflict. Use of such basic skills can sometimes make a surprising difference in transforming a potentially hostile situation into a win-win situation.

Transforming power is using the higher levels of one person's consciousness to reach another person's consciousness. The object is to avoid violence, but more basically to improve the mutual empathy among persons. Even in the most hostile situations, it's shown that there is available to each person an inner reservoir of strength and an energizing spirit to accomplish this. These techniques work well in many ordinary, real-life situations. They are easily learned. They're another example of how relatively simple concepts and practices can make a substantial difference in the quality of life.

A Composite View?

In the above, we've noted the diverse expressions of religious and rehabilitation groups to guide people to a better life. The Old and

New Testaments, the Buddhist Way, and the Quaker AVP all fit well together. It appears that there is a universal inclination to formulate such guidelines. Even fraternal organizations do it, to suit their specific aims. Witness, the Boy Scouts of America. Their Scout Law is another current example of crisp personal guidelines: "A Scout is trustworthy, helpful, friendly, courteous, kind, obedient, cheerful, thrifty, brave, clean, and reverent."

Doesn't it seem that these are all facets of the same thing? Isn't this just the different views, from different perspectives, of a single fundamental phenomenon? Isn't it the composite view, and more besides, that is the reality?

To understand the composite, in the hurly-burly of daily life, is a tall order. Again, however, we suggest that all of these guidelines are related to the goal of moving each individual to greater and greater consciousness. The three components of empathy, caring love, and kindness, seem to be an essential part, - indeed, a fountainhead, of every set of guidelines.

In any case, we need to pick some specific action guidelines, or use all of the above. Rather than drifting aimlessly, we use such guidelines to set our course, and measure our progress in reference to them. For each of us, the selection is a personal choice, opportunity, and responsibility.

8.5 BUILDING THE EARTH

Living fully finally must involve a heightened awareness of our responsibility to all the peoples of this earth, both present and future. Poverty, exploitation, and all manner of social injustice still abound. We also see and become concerned with eroded farm lands, dying lakes, urban slums, dumping beds in oceans, and the pile-up of radioactive wastes with half-lives in the tens of thousands of years. We see that personal profit and short-term gain have been made at the expense of exploited people and the long-term expense of the earth itself. Our stewardship of this miraculous gift, our earth, is often to our shame.

Waking Up

We must not be complacent about all this. We need to 'be in touch with our anger', to rouse ourselves to caring and working for solutions. Persons of good will need to draw together in their anger, lift their group voice, and find the mutual strength to work for needed change. But great consciousness is needed, nevertheless, to prevent anger from taking control and shutting out the humanity of the opponents.

Too much anger degenerates to rage, with its inability to communicate; this leads to violence and no solutions. Rather the anger must be recognized, and used to generate the words that help in understanding the situation. The motivation must be channeled so as to build consciousness on both sides of the issue.

We need to claim our God-given right to be fully human; we need to claim the ability to have full consciousness, in space and time. We need to claim the gifts that come with that consciousness, despite the many obstacles we encounter. With confidence in that inherent ability, and in the Divine Providence that wills our true fulfillment, we can enjoy moving forward. Committing ourselves to a harmony with that divine plan, we can proceed. Even despite pain (and we can expect more than we'd like), we can live fully. Sure, some things are beyond our ability to change. To some extent, we have to leave some long range changes in God's hands; but where we have minds, hearts, hands, and feet to offer, we are happier in applying them to the task, even if the results are temporarily small.

As the process of evolution continues, what can we hope for? We can perceive, over the centuries, something akin to what happens in every life. The very young child thinks only of himself. Later he comprehends the existence of a few persons besides himself, and he optimizes some combination of his welfare and theirs. His circle of friends grows; he tries to optimize the good of his family, his school, or perhaps his tribe or nation. Similarly, but over many generations, we can hope for growth in the average levels of consciousness of humankind as a whole. We look for a gradually wider distribution of consciousness, where more people think empathetically, involving more other people and over longer time periods. We can expect a clearer realization of our purpose to preserve and personally enhance the overall on-going creation. We each need to contribute to achieving that goal.

Steady Construction

Building of the earth starts with the people of the earth. This construction must be earned. The 'world-economy' in consciousness is improved or weakened by the daily decisions of every person. The 'coin' in this economy is empathy; and our 'standard of living' is measured in acts of kindness. The 'gross national product' depends on everyone's productivity.

The most common way of improving this economy is by our compassionate relations to those around us. Broken-hearted or broken-spirited or poverty-stricken persons are as ordinary as the common cold. Everything from anxiety, personal failures, and feelings of inadequacy, through conflict and violence, to physical, psychological, and economic tragedies, is an everyday part of our world. Often, simply by being a sympathetic listener, or extending the hand of understanding and friendship, we can contribute to a healing. Often, we have the opportunity to do more.

We (all of us) build the earth in collaboration with imperfect people. Every one of us, of course, is far from perfect; we accept that, and the blemishes in others as well. Rather than rejecting people because of their defects, we realize their possession of some valuable capabilities, and their potential for the development of others. We are grateful for what we each have; we build upon that; and we use what we have as much as possible.

The key, of course, is in the fundamental option of the ordinary person. Increasing consciousness, as a fundamental option, leads to a philosophy of service to all others, for their growth, as well as our own. More and more, we can see the development of the idea of the 'voluntary servant', who is totally free, and master of his own destiny, and yet dedicated to serving others. The noted Catholic psychologist, Eugene Kennedy, describes this emerging phenomenon as follows:

> Servanthood does not ask us to subject ourselves to the control of some higher authority; it invites us to commit ourselves with as much awareness as possible to the design of our own religious destiny. Servanthood is an invitation to take our existence seriously and not to let someone else supervise it or control it too closely. We have witnessed the death of that blind obedience that matched the model of monarchy. It is an achievement of Christian development that we return now to the state of being servants who are not slaves but persons who realize fully the dignity of their calling and of their obedience to the needs of mankind. Servanthood is a voluntary state; its richness flows from the freedom with which people join themselves to it. The

meaning of servanthood lies in the power of love that is its only energy as well as the only sign of the Spirit that is completely trustworthy.[12]

All of us must also enlist in the fight for social justice. As we discussed earlier, there are many areas where each of us can be concerned and make a difference. Discrimination of all kinds, and separatism in its many forms need to be exposed and empathetically argued against. The steady pounding of millions of little hammers can gradually reshape our world.

Technologically-oriented humankind gradually perceives the tremendous sociological damage that can result from the narrow use of wealth and technology. Gradually, we find that the view is broadened, and a new awareness of reality sets in. The result is a development of a social responsibility on the part of more individuals, institutions, industrial firms, and governments. Hopefully, that clarity of responsibility generates a greater commitment to work with and for others in the considerate building of the earth.

The Possible World

We must be optimistic if we are to progress. We must look forward to the day when a significantly larger percentage of the peoples on the earth have developed a world consciousness, involving empathy, caring love, and kindness for all. The world culture would then support the emphasis on the inherent dignity of every person. The priorities of persons and institutions would then shift significantly towards the common purpose, - of building the earth for all persons, with liberty and justice.

This empathy for and service to all in the world community may be aided by the continuing rapid progress in those forms of communication which bring people closer, help us to understand one another, and enable us to share in the experiences of one another in real time. The attitudes of persons is key, and those attitudes may be improved by easier and more complete information flows.

We already find that even relatively crude computer-aided conferencing facilitates cooperation among people who otherwise would be separated by social barriers. Looking ahead, one can see the possibility of many more persons participating interactively and contributing creatively, each being an intelligent node of worldwide communications networks. George Bugliarello, President of Polytechnic Institute of N.Y., puts it this way:

> Networks with nodes throughout our society become a far more comprehensive, sensitive, and swift device for addressing social, political, economic, or other kinds of issues than anything available today...millions of nodes tuned to problem solving represent a quantum step in the mental capacity of our species...Networks will lead to a new morality because they will put us in a broader context, more connected to one another across national and ideological boundaries, and more connected to our environment on this planet...Networks will integrate knowledge, intelligence and the new moral sense toward the achievement of new goals.[13]

With very rapid communication and improved ability to feel, perceive, and understand worldwide, a greater awareness of all people as sacred persons could result. In time, we can hope that a greater realization of the sacredness of the individual would foster more individual respect, freedom, initiative, and creativity. This would be accompanied by concern for the total population. The primary goals would include that no person need starve or be sick and unattended, or be ignorant, or be destitute, or live among the scars of pollution that were caused by overly-selfish exploitation of the earth.

In this evolution, we would look for the preservation of the opportunities of private initiative, and the rewards resulting therefrom; but at the same time there would be a steady movement towards a more equitable distribution and sharing of the earth's wealth. We would expect the standard to become that of socially responsible domestic and international industry. Finally, international governmental cooperation would likewise reflect this keen awareness of the personhood of the occupants of all countries, rather than the economic or military competition among them.

Overly optimistic? We think not, in the long run. Real progress may take many generations to achieve. However, each challenging step can have its rewards. Without optimism there can only be indifference leading to despair; and the human race is far from ready for that. On the contrary there is faith in the faintly-known forces that move our evolution to higher states of consciousness and hence to progress in building the earth. Moreover, it's in this kind of effort that humankind finally finds more lasting satisfaction. To use our transforming power to move the world even a small step towards compassion and peace, is to live more fully. As Gutierrez says:

> Consequently, when we assert that man fulfills himself by continuing the work of creation by means of his labor, we are saying that he places himself, by this very fact, within an all embracing salvific process. To work, to transform the world, is to become a man and to build the human community; it is also to save. Likewise, to struggle against misery and exploitation and to build a just society is already to be part of the saving action, which is moving towards its complete fulfillment.[14]

Thus, the practical occasions for growth in consciousness, and hence the 'building of the earth', are everywhere, every day. It is only in these real life conflicts and difficult choices that growth is possible. Every challenge is therefore an opportunity to foster such growth. In that way, we each contribute to the broad evolutionary birthing of consciousness, that ultimately is the birth of the Spirit of God on earth. We each have that essential, irreplaceable role, - to make our small contribution. In so doing, we reap real joy, - an inner satisfaction that we are striving to become all that we can be.

So it is our expectation that real progress can be made, even in our life-times. We further hope that, ultimately, this process of birth, helped in a small way by each of us, spread over millions of years, will approach its beautiful completion, as the 'kingdom of God' on earth.

REFERENCES

[1]P. D. Ouspensky, *The Fourth Way*, Vintage Books, New York, 1971, p. 48.
[2]P. D. Ouspensky, *loc. cit.*, p. 313.
[3]Huston Smith, *The Religions of Man*, Harper and Row, New York, 1958, p. 96.
[4]P. D. Ouspensky, *loc. cit.*, p. 260.

[5]R.P. McBrien, *Catholicism*, Winston Press, Minneapolis, Mn.,1980, pp. 777–783.

[6]Huston Smith, *loc. cit.*, pp. 116–123.

[7]Bukkyo Dendo Kyokai, *The Teaching of Buddha*, Kosaido Printing Co., Ltd., Tokyo, Japan, 1985, pp. 38–43, 166–168.

[8]Monika K. Hellwig, "As God is Good" *America*, February 14, 1987, p. 145.

[9]Thomas Merton, *New Seeds of Contemplation*, New Directions, New York, 1961, p. 72.

[10]Alternatives to Violence Project, Inc., 15 Rutherford Place, New York, N.Y., 10003.

[11]Lawrence S.Apsey, J.Bristol, and K.Eppler,*Transforming Power For Peace*, Religious Education Committee of Friends General Conference, Philadelphia, Pa, 1981.

[12]Eugene Kennedy, *The Now and Future Church*, Doubleday & Co., Garden City, N.Y. 1985, p. 188.

[13]George Bugliarello, "A Global Network Emerges; It Will Lead to Hyperintelligence", *Science Digest*, March 1984, p. 49.

[14]Gustavo Gutierrez, *A Theology of Liberation*, Orbis Books, Maryknoll, N.Y., 1973, p. 159.

OTHER SOURCES

H. Kung, *Does God Exist?*, Doubleday & Co., Garden City, N.Y.,1980.

M. Scott Peck, *The Road Less Traveled*, Simon and Schuster, N.Y., 1978.

James Carroll, *A Terrible Beauty*, Newman Press, N.Y., 1973, p.130.

J.F. Donceel, *America*, Feb 2, 1985, pp. 81–83.

K.E.Untener, "Local Church and Universal Church", *America*, Oct. 13, 1984.

Jose de Vinck, *The Virtue of Sex*, Abbey Press, St. Meinrad, Indiana, 1966.

Lewis Browne, *The World's Great Scriptures*, Macmillan Co., New York, 1946, p. XV.

H.Von Campenhausen, *The Formation of the Christian Bible*, Fortress Press, Philadelphia, Pa., 1972.

Taikichi Irie and Shigeru Aoyame, *Buddhist Images*, Hoikusha Publishing Co., Ltd., Osaka, Japan, Second Edition, 1971.

H. Kung, *Signposts for the Future*, Doubleday & Co. N.Y., 1978.

W. Marxsen, "The Resurrection of Jesus of Nazareth", Fortress Press, *Maryknoll Formation Journal*, Spring-Summer '84, p. 51.

Jane I. Smith, "Islam: Fulfillment Through Submission", *National Catholic Reporter*, November 28, 1986, pp. 9–10.

Thomas Berry, "Our Children: Their Future," *the little magazine*, Bear and Co., Vol. 1, Number 10, p. 10.

Dennis O'Brien, "One, Holy, Catholic, and Somewhat Infallible", *America*, April 4, 1987, p. 278.